To Amy, Chloe, Titus, and Silas … in case you didn't know, you made my life.

To Ron: you crazy old Texan; you taught me more than you'll ever know.

To the people of The Journey Community Church in Conifer, Colorado: you guys are so easy to love.

To my team, my best friends: if all this ever falls apart, let's sell cars together.

For those in ministry in any way, shape, or form … you are my heroes.

And for Gloria … you were right after all.

Contents

Introduction

A Little Armed Robbery for Jesus

MY FRIENDS AND I had spent the better part of two months meeting and planning the church. We were all tired and pretty angry because not much was being decided. You see, we all came from different parts of the country and different churches, so naturally, we had very different ideas of how an Acts 2 church would work today and not look like a cult. After one rather intense disagreement over how we would actually reach our community, I had, had enough!

I blurted out, "We couldn't knock over a 7-Eleven together, let alone start a church! We would all be arguing about who would hold the gun, who would drive the getaway car, and if we should grab the burritos in the process!"

I excused myself, left my apartment, and made my way upstairs to the roof of our building. It's a flat roof, and the door lock had been broken years ago. That roof offered a nice view of the mountains and isolation from life. I felt like we were spinning our wheels. I would love to say that I prayed and heard God, but I just stood there for fifteen minutes or so and then returned to my team.

Back in my apartment, to my amazement, there was laughter coming from inside. When I opened the door, I was met with a very electric room. One of the people there handed me a pad of paper outlined with very distinct plans on how they would rob a 7-Eleven, complete with time lines, job descriptions, and assignments. It was super-detailed, and if executed, I am sure we would have made off with all $25 they keep in the register.

That was the first time the team worked right. I realized that we needed to take on every task the same way. After all, we are in the business of stealing. We are in the high-stakes game of stealing back the hearts of people and returning them to their Father.

This book is part story and part life lessons lived by a group of friends who took off after their calling. We are in no way educated experts. We are, in fact, very undereducated. When we started planting this church, not one person on the senior staff had a Bible college degree. In fact, two key leaders have only GEDs—but never think that we do not love learning. We read everything on church growth and leadership. We also steal ideas and programs from the best churches in the country.

We are in no way a megachurch. We would love to be. However, in the town we are in, the population is only about nine thousand. In the two and a half years our church has existed, we have grown to well over five hundred people every weekend. Our goal is to get to 50 percent of the total population. In addition to the struggle of starting in a tiny town, we had absolutely no funding or outside support. On the day we started, we had $224 among the thirteen of us. Like so many of you, we had to fight our way into existence. But what I feel we do offer is hope— hope for the church in a small town that wants to do big things, hope for those of us who have little or no support to get off the runway and fly, and hope for some innovative ideas on how to reach people who are very tough to get to.

Conifer is a mountain community about forty-five minutes outside of Denver. There are two distinct groups of people here. Some have been living up here for years and want to be left alone. They cut their own wood, have snow plows on their trucks, and have ZZ Top beards. And that's just the women. I kid … kind of. We have a friend named Chainsaw Bob, and he is the real-life Jeremiah Johnson. He smells like Marlboro Lights and gasoline. The man is just cool. Then there are a growing number of younger families moving from the city to raise their families in a smaller community. It makes for an interesting mix. I know for me, it was a culture shock.

I'm a city boy. In reality, I'm the last guy on earth God should have sent here, but God has a sense of humor and a sense of destiny. I must admit that I was dragged here by God, but now I couldn't imagine living anywhere else. I have found home.

This book has no real order. I just really want to share our story, thoughts, and ideas with others who are starting out. I believe the kingdom is helped the more we talk about our journeys toward fulfilling our missions. It's just stuff we stole from other churches that shared their stories. So buckle up, and we will talk as men talk. I'll tell you the story of how a diner opened hearts, an odd job business almost got us arrested, how movies on the football field made us known, and how a race car is helping single moms.

Maybe you'll get some ideas to help you in your own towns. Maybe you'll laugh and identify with our struggles, or maybe some of you will see that if God came through for us, then it is safe for you to get out of the boat and walk toward Jesus.

Remember, there are no small churches—just small visions. So as William Benjamin Basil King said, "Let's be bold, and mighty forces will come to our aid!"

Medicaid, Food Stamps, and Other Perks of Starting a Church

"If God only gave me a clear sign, like making a large deposit in my name at a Swiss bank."

-Woody Allen

AH, THE STARTUP CHURCH and money. It's so hard to get those two in the same room together. It's great if you have a church or ministry funding you, but what about those of us who just feel called and don't have access to cash or support? You could reach out to Christian friends and family who have money, but that didn't work for our team. Sure, we could get support if we were willing to build a church in the "darkest of Africa," but no one wanted to finance a church startup in the "darkest of Colorado." Sure, there were a few churches and other ministry avenues that were willing to discuss helping us, but in the end, the strings that came with the help made the offer too steep to accept.

Some of us will remember the phrase that well-meaning people tell us as we embark on an endeavor for Christ.

They say, "Don't give it a second thought, brother. Where God guides, he provides."

I had a rather well-known Christian TV personality tell me that once. A year later, I watched two of his telethons yield very little support. After that, it seemed his theology crumbled, and his TV ministry ended. Now, I do believe that God can do anything; however, I also believe that many times, God leaves huge obstacles in our way just to teach us to become stronger and smarter and to grow in our faith. I believe that where God guides, I must go—and if needed, cut a new path through ways never traveled. I had a lieutenant in the fire department who had a favorite saying when things got tough: "Pray to God! But row for shore all the same." In other words, we have some responsibility to do our part as well.

For the Journey church team, we hit our first wall instantly with a thud. We had no funding at all. We were also super-young and very broke. Most of our credit was bad or nonexistent. I mean it—credit so bad that stores wouldn't even accept our cash. Add to that the ridiculous costs associated with starting a church: rental costs for a place to meet, flyers and posters to get the word out, maybe even a mail-out, lights, sound systems, and my favorite expense, media equipment—things like computers, software, and cameras. And don't forget the mother of all expenses—projectors. If you are about to start a church and haven't priced these bad boys, then get ready to pee your pants and forget your name for half an hour. It's like getting tazed. These things must be made out of panda. But wait. It gets better. You need two. That way both sides of the auditorium can have a screen. They also don't respond well when they're dropped, have coffee spilled on them, or people use them as a step—all of which we found out within a month of the purchase.

So after all our wealthier relatives told us no about helping us with cash, we all got jobs and began to live on as little as possible, putting the rest toward buying things to start the church. This worked fine for a while until we began to see some cracks in our system. You see, we all now worked fifty to sixty hours a week, and we began to drift from our vision. Life began to take over. To make things harder, most of us worked physically demanding jobs. Several of us worked on a horse ranch; others worked for a carpet cleaning business and a party supply company delivering and setting up seven-hundred-pound bounce houses and such. It's easy to see why we had very little energy to sit down and plan a church at 11:00 every night after work. I know I really began to have doubts about how we would keep the steam hot and pumping while spreading ourselves out too thin.

This came to a head one Thanksgiving day. We all had the day off and wanted to spend it together. After a nice meal, the conversation began to turn toward the frustration everyone was feeling. We each felt disconnected. One person brought up that it would be great if we all worked at the same job. Then we could work, plan the church, and bond as teammates at the same time. We talked for hours that day and decided that we needed to find a way to make a living together.

In my life, I have had the opportunities to work many different part-time jobs. For some reason, business always came easy to me. I enjoy the entrepreneurial spirit. It makes sense to me. To add to that, I was blessed to work and learn from some very successful business people. As that conversation progressed, someone noticed a TV commercial talking about a junk-hauling business that employed "college hunks." I suggested we start an odd jobs company called "Ministries Hunks" as a joke. No one laughed. It only took thirty minutes for that joke to become a real idea and plan. With great fanfare, we all gave our notices and quit our jobs.

Now, let me take this moment to tell you that we got hammered by all our families for taking this risk. I really understood their concerns. I felt them as well. Having said that, I also know that it is impossible to steal second base with your foot on first. I'm a gambler by nature anyway. I also firmly believe that if you're going to build anything great with your life, then you will have some defining moments—times when you push all your chips into the middle of the table and play the hand you have been dealt. This was that moment for our church.

Just before Christmas, we launched the Journey Odd Jobs Company. We took out ads in the newspaper and on Denver's Craigslist. We used a credit card and charged $100 worth of flyers to hand out in store parking lots. We even got a call the very first day! Someone needed an old TV moved down four flights of stairs to their dumpster. We made a cool $20 for that. We began to do moving jobs, lawn work, painting, house cleaning, and snow shoveling. The funny thing was that we really had no idea how to do anything when we started. We would get a call asking if we knew how to do something like putting in a French drain in someone's yard. "You bet!" was always our answer. We would schedule a time for the following day to come give them a bid. Then we would hang up and look on YouTube to see what a French drain was and how to install it. YouTube saved our butts so many times, we lost count. We would then call a few professional places and get a rough bid so we knew what the going rate was, and in turn, cut their bid in half. And that was our estimate.

We also became very close friends with some guys who worked at Home Depot and Lowe's. Did you know that they offer all kinds of classes there? We attended a ton of them. When things really exceeded our understanding, we simply would hire a professional to do it for us, all the while standing over his shoulder watching and making notes. In retrospect, we must have looked incredibly creepy to those guys, but we had to watch closely in order to understand how to do it ourselves next time. Within no time, we could install sprinkler systems, fix boiler issues, and repair almost any plumbing problem you could think of. Landscape, paint, sheet rock, tape and float … we did it all.

It took us about three months to really get going full steam, and by then we realized we were bringing in four times the money that we had all made separately. And all throughout the workday, we bonded as a team and talked about the church we wanted to build. It was really working out better than we could have imagined. It's funny how sweat and hard work can bring together a group of people!

Now around this time, we began to get calls from realty companies and banks to do what was called "trash outs." When a home gets repossessed, many people tend to leave the house trashed and dirty. Our job was to come in and clean these wrecked properties. This was very profitable, but turned out to be harder emotionally than you might expect. We cleaned out the last of people's memories. Many would leave pictures and letters behind. We sat in one home for an hour and read through a husband and wife's correspondence as they ended their relationship. He was serving in Iraq, and she had found someone new in the United States. They had two small, beautiful kids together, and this new little family that was just starting out was over already. In another room of the house, on the back of the closet door, written in red crayon were the words "I miss my dad." It was clear that a child had written it. That kind of daily find wrecked us in a good way.

God began to use these trash-outs to increase our passion for reaching the hurting. Each day, we would read letters and journals left behind from real people recording the frustrations so many of us feel. In one home we cleaned, someone had spray-painted "God hates me" on the living room wall. In the middle of it, they had taken their eviction notice and stabbed it to the wall with a kitchen knife. Ripped-up wedding pictures and broken memories are what we saw all too often. When we would leave job sites, instead of the usual jokes and conversations, there was a lot more silence and staring out windows.

Christ was doing surgery on our insides; he was making our hearts grow. And even though we were being paid for these jobs, we all felt like God was putting us through some advanced training sessions in understanding the people he loves so much. It may seem strange, but it was those moments that made us feel more urgency and empowerment to engage in people's nightmares and bring them hope.

Even though we made a good amount of money, we still needed more to buy the equipment we needed. Some of our guys literally went dumpster diving behind music stores and dug out speakers and cords that had seen better days. Adam, one of our teaching pastors and resident MacGyver, spent hours with the Internet, duct tape, and a soldering iron learning how to fix the junk we pulled out of trash cans. We were amazed at what we could find in dumpsters and alleys. Denver is also a big city for garage bands. And as anyone knows who watches VH1's Behind the Music, almost all bands break up. When local bands end, they sell all their stuff on Craigslist in a huff and in a hurry. We watched for these "breakup sales" and got really good stuff for very little. We got our soundboard because our friend, a local bookie, talked us into giving him $50 for a "sure thing." He bet on three long shot games. He won on all of them and gave us $550 back. I'm not promoting gambling to start a church or get equipment, but I find it beyond funny that our first soundboard was procured because the Denver Nuggets covered the point spread.

In the end, that odd jobs company gave us the ability to start our church. If we couldn't afford something, we used credit cards to get it. I know many of you will have issues with people using credit to start a church. I didn't, and it worked for us, so let's just leave the MasterCard debate for another time. Let's just say we needed the miles. Anyway, the simple fact is that hard work and ingenuity pays off. So many churches never make it out of someone's living room because the people behind the church are waiting for the cavalry to ride in with a checkbook and rescue us. I believe that the local church needs leaders need a "never say die" attitude toward their calling. I believe we would all see bigger things happen when church leaders decide they will build a church on our own steam for a while if they have to.

Today, we have a great, growing church full of people who would literally give you the shirt off their back if they saw you needed it. I love the people in this church and community. They are awesome. But I will always believe that God sent them to our church because he saw a bunch of selfless, hardworking kids who got the steam hot and the train moving when there was no one. Sure, we had to sell our cars and some possessions. And yes, we had to work long hours, learn new skills, and sweat buckets. We even sold our plasma. Yes, they buy it. But we found that God does provide a way for us to fulfill our mission. In that same process, we saw God build into us the confidence to take any hill and fight the unknown. Don't let money issues scare you. There is a ton of money out there. You do know they print more of it every day.

God will get on your side when he sees that you're willing to take the fight to the next level and go get what it is you need. Today's church leaders need to be fighters. We should be a worthy enemy to our old foe, the devil. To compete at this level, we have to play the full nine innings—the entire game—full speed to the end. Start strong, break some rules, and blaze your own trail into your calling. You might be surprised what ideas God has hidden in you when you have to dig for them.

The Need for a Body Count

You had me at "Hell, no."

ANYONE WHO HAS EVER tried to build a church from the ground up knows the feeling of watching the people walk in the door at your very first service. You are thrilled that someone showed; however, the look on their faces when they realize that they are one of the three people who showed up makes you feel sorry for them. Their eyes say, "There is no way I'm sneaking out early from this service." Yikes! Most handle it in stride, but the truth is that people feel better in crowds. Lost in the mass of bodies, we can be observers, not participants.

When you start a church, you have to go through this awkward stage. I for one had planned to avoid it and start with several hundred like Rick Warren. I had read his book, The Purpose Driven Church, and thought his way was and still is (by far) the best. If you start with hundreds, you can leap over the worst phrase a church leader has to say to guests: "*Come in.*

Yes, you're the only one today." I have had to say that, and honestly, I would rather pee on an electric fence. And yes, I've done both—several times, actually. Anyhow, it's just part of the fun of church planting, so embrace it, and have fun. As Shakespeare said, "Ambition should be made of sterner stuff."

Now, there are some things we learned in the trials to get people in our doors—lessons that you may find helpful to increase your body count on the weekend. You should remember that just because the church is front and center in your mind and your team members' minds does not mean your community knows or even thinks about it. This sounds simple, but it caught us by surprise. We were consumed with the church twenty-four/seven. So when others didn't come through the doors, we realized that we had to do more than make a sign for Sundays. To grow our church, we had to fish with a net, not a pole.

First, we made cards with our church's name and website to hand to anyone we had conversations with. The first card we handed out had way too much info. It was like we were trying to close the deal with a card printed front, back, and sides. It had information on every program we planned to do: youth, children's church, missions, staff, service times, education background or lack thereof, dates for Christ's return, DNA results of leaders, and of course, our mission statement. It was just too much, and we had little to no response. We began to see the website as the net we could cast into our community. The truth of the matter is that almost every person who visits your church is doing so for the second time. The first visit happens when they visit your church's web page. In the age in which we live, it is the front door to our churches. This needs to be a place to show them who we are. We made our site easy to navigate and full of pictures. People need to see others to feel safe. If you seem small and unprofessional, they will click off. So put your best foot forward. In the data we have recorded, I can tell you the four big things people look at first.

The sermon matters. If your speaker sucks, it's over. Sorry, but it's the reality of our profession. Gift, in this area, matters. If you're not that gifted, work at it. Use illustrations. Try harder. I fall into that category. I have to work at it harder than most to do it well. If you're good, get great. If you're bad, get good. It is necessary. People go straight to hear if the speaker is good, passionate, or interesting. The game ends here if you cannot communicate well. Speakers today must be good at their craft.

Early in my development, I was told that ten hours was an adequate amount of time to prepare a sermon. When I relayed this to my mentors, they said, "Michael, you need to make it twenty hours, and you'll do better." I was young enough to take them at their word, and that is what I do to this day. It has helped me to no end.

But back on topic—you have to put up at least one podcast even before you launch so people can hear the goods. This presents a problem for young preachers, because many have never had the chance to record even one sermon. I had taught at other churches but found that I wanted to present a sample sermon on what this local church could be. So we recorded a sermon in my wet, scary basement. It was good, but in all the areas I made jokes or used humor, it sounded dead, because no one laughed. It also sounded muffled and weird—kind of like it was recorded in some creepy guy's basement. You kept waiting to hear someone yell, "It rubs the lotion on its skin, or else it gets the hose again." My media guys said they had an idea and asked for a day to work on it to see if they could make it sound legit.

The next morning, they played the remastered version. Wow! What a difference! They had changed the audio to make it sound like I was preaching in a big auditorium. That alone helped tons. But they also added laugh tracks when I made jokes. It was amazing! It sounded real! It made us sound the way we wanted to be. We only did that once to give people the idea of what it would sound like in an auditorium, but it was enough to get us going.

The second web page people looked at was about our worship and music. We had no worship team yet—just the leader. Sterling, our worship leader, made a playlist of fifty songs he loved to worship God to. He listed artists he liked and influences they had on him. It was like a mix tape dedicated to the people you're trying to win over. Look, I grew up in the '80s, and mix tapes were the way to the hearts! And of course, who doesn't love David Crowder Band, Hillsong, and U2? We let people know that because we were a new church, we need help in that area. People really responded in a big way.

The third most viewed page had to do with children's church. I cannot over-emphasize how big a deal this is. We really didn't do a good enough job making children's church an awesome program that first year. In fact, a young couple who had been coming to church for several months were the ones who helped us see this clearly. After they hadn't come for a month, we knew that maybe they had moved on.

One day, the woman sent an e-mail. She was super-nice and complimented everything about our church. She loved the teaching, music, and media. She loved the outreach we had in our community. But they had found another church because, as she put it, "you guys treat children's church like a day care or an afterthought." She reminded us that children matter to God too, and we should try to put as much effort into them as we do everyone else. Ouch! It stung so badly because she was completely right. We made sure to give children's church more leadership, time, and money.

As we did that, we began to see that kids were actually the reason many people chose our church. Many of our committed core members said that they only became fans because of how passionate their kids were about coming to church. Of course, you have to get creative to get there—especially if you're meeting in a rented place like a theater or school. Our children's church was held in the wrestling room at the high school. It smelled like sweat and butt every Sunday morning. We had to clean it and make it appealing to get kids to come. We have found that inflatable bounce houses work best at getting kids out of their parent's arms and into our world.

And last, prospective church members look for the youth programs. Now, there are different schools of thought about how long you go until you have a youth program. I believe you need to launch it at the same time as your church. With giving going way down in churches, it seems that the youth pastor position is becoming more and more expendable—especially with smaller churches. I really think you have to keep that position alive. Find a way. Teens are the adults of tomorrow, and we can't let little things like no money or a place to meet stop us. The head youth pastor in our church is a kid named Cortland. He got on a bus in Kansas at seventeen and showed up at our door. He smelled like pot, patchouli, and taco seasoning. He was an angry young man. Now he is a stunningly good leader. He is twenty-one, married, and showers every day. Thank you, Jesus! He also fights with me weekly on needing more money for the rapidly growing youth group. He carries the banner for the youth program and will not be denied. That's what you want in a youth pastor: a person who knows the high stakes our kids are facing and is willing to even get in the leader's face to get the money and help they need. Truthfully, Cortland drives me crazy, but I must admit that he has my respect, and I love him like a son.

Okay, so that's what people look for at your website. Your site is the foyer to your church. They will decide right there if you're worth the risk. That site will either lead them to your doors or to another church's website. Work on it. Add to it. Read it for spelling or informational errors. Steal, steal, steal from churches that do it better than you. We take a ton from about fifty other churches. Is it wrong? Who cares? I don't. Just copy those who do it better than you, and if they get mad, tell them to chill out and realize that stealing ideas is the highest form of flattery. Most churches are super-cool about it.

All right, back to getting them to the website—and in turn, the door. We made and printed two hundred small fourteen-by-eighteen posters and put them up all over town. We used stock photos of people visiting with each other and crowds listening to a speaker. Pictures matter. On everything you print, you should have faces. We announced that a new church was launching.

During this time, we heavily monitored the traffic on our website. We tried to average fifty new hits a day. If one poster got very little response, we would change it until it got the desired hits. It is a never-ending tweaking process. We also left thousands of yellow handwritten Post-it notes that said, "Just thought you'd like this—Journeyfoothills.com." We would sign our name and stick it on people's doors. Just plain curiosity made most go to the computer and check out the web address on the note.

If I had to guess which idea brought the most bodies through the door, I would say that one by far. Sure, we got a few ticked off people who didn't like the way we did it, but the massive response we got dwarfed the angry birds. It's a lesson we had to learn quickly. Whenever we tried to reach people, we made some mad. Get used to it. It's all part of the process.

Now, let's talk about stalking people. The reality is that when people show up for a service, we want them to return. For lack of a better term, we call it our "capture rate." As of now, for every ten people who visit our church, seven become regular attendees. Our goal is to stay over a 70 percent capture rate all the time. Now, when there are only thirty people, this can be an awkward thing to connect after a service to "feel them out." Some people make a mad dash out, walking in zigzags to avoid our staff.

Early on, we had a "take no prisoners" approach. The final prayer of the service was the time our staff moved to all the exits to be able to catch and connect with every visitor. Most loved to chat, but those who did not made us feel confused. Do you let them go or chase them down like a lion stalking prey in the Serengeti? You know, to let them know we care a lot … maybe too much. We finally came to the conclusion that not everyone wants to connect the day they visit. We have become better at letting the bolters go without chasing them to the parking lot with coffee and guest cards.

In the end, we try to talk to everyone who seems interested and curious and let the others know we are always here when they want to talk. We do one follow-up call that week thanking them for trying us out, and if they gave us their e-mail address, we include them in our church event e-mails. But that's where it stops. We want to give people room to make a decision for themselves.

Oh yes, one final thought: in setting up for our first service, we set up four hundred chairs. The argument was that it was showing God how much faith we had. I'm sure it did. However, when only three people came, it showed us how big of a lame-sauce idea that was. We found that if a room feels empty, then it feels awkward. We began to space chairs with about two feet between them and set up everything near the stage. We turned off lights in the very back to close off the rest of the room.

Over time, as we had to put out more and more chairs, we were able to see the church fill up the room. I guess my caution is that the space needs to feel somewhat full even if it's not. Have your team sit throughout the auditorium. Get them to invite people if they can. Use guilt or bribes.

One guy on our team is a real chick magnet. He used to have seven to ten college girls at every service. They wanted him, not God, but we were all happy with him using his looks to increase the crowd, if only just for filling seats. It won't take long until the chairs fill up on their own. But it will take forever if your room always feels empty.

Well, that's how we got the bus moving. The truth is, however, that all these ideas have run their course. Church growth engines are like tires. Each one only has so much tread. But these helped us get moving. Over time, we have had way more success with some more novel but risky ideas. The truth we all know is that every community has its walls and challenges. Each church has to meet people where they are at. For us, one of the biggest ways into the lives of these mountain communities was to go through, of all places … Hollywood.

The Cinematic Adventures

"I don't know! I'm making this up as I go!"
-Indiana Jones, Raiders of the Lost Ark

LOVE THE STORY of the Trojan horse. After a ten-year siege by the Greeks on Troy, there had been no progress. So the Greeks gave Troy a gift of a giant wooden horse and pretended to sail away. Troy brought it into the city, not knowing that inside the gift were thirty Greek soldiers. Then, under the cover of night, the hidden soldiers emerged from the belly of the horse and opened the front gate to the city, letting in the remaining army that had returned in the night. By the next morning, the war was over—all because the Greeks got proximity to open the walls.

Say what you want, but if we are going to reach people far from God, we are going to have to deal with walls as tall and strong as those at Troy. Like the Greeks, we may need to rethink how we try scaling these walls. For most people, the world is a brutal and unforgiving place. From a very early age, we all begin to erect a personal defense system to protect us from each other and even God. So walking up to people and going straight into a Christian sales pitch usually turns out as well as eating Taco Bell that's been left out all night. Yeah, it normally ends rough.

As we began to build our church, we realized that we were gathering Christians, but very few that were far from God. I have worked for and with churches that claimed to be about lost people, but never really reached any. It's a cool thing to say in our mission statement, but to do it feels almost impossible. As our team began to discuss how to overcome this obstacle, we realized a few things had to change in our thinking.

First, we decided we needed proximity without agenda. I have found that the longer I have been a Christian, the fewer non-Christians I know. It's not that I don't like them; church has just become the place we all find our friends, mates, and social interaction. Sure, I try to spark up relationships when I'm out and about, but inevitably, people ask what I do for a living. The moment they know I'm a pastor, they look at me like I'm going to take up an offering.

People have preconceived ideas of Christians from TV evangelists, church scandals, and of course, politics. They are convinced that we are all right-wing conservatives, that we hate abortion, hate all gays, and homeschool our children. We pray before every bite and say "bless you" after all sneezes. They think we think sex is bad, that we never use bad words, and that we sacrifice goats on the Blood Moon. It's just crazy. We all know we only sacrifice chickens on the Blood Moon. (No e-mails … it's a joke.) But in order to show people that we are all the same, we needed to be friends first before we could even think of talking about God.

Second, we decided to attend to our community instead of asking our community to attend our church. We began to send staff to every community event we could find. Some went to town hall meetings; others joined the Chamber of Commerce, and the guys went to every community sports event we could find. We even entered a float in the local Christmas parade. Last year, we won the prize for Most Creative Float! Yeah, we bring our A-game all day, every day. A few staff members went to local bars on the same night every week to establish friendships. Sterling and Brian began playing pick-up games at nearby basketball courts.

We began to make some real non-church friends. It was a staff requirement to get involved with people who were not Christians and to in no way let them know we were church leaders. On a side note, I think it helped us more than them. In church work, we can lose touch with what people really deal with on a daily basis. We have to feel like the average Janes and Joes in the world. Talking about life, marriage, and jobs helped us reconnect with the people Christ loves so much. I guess the best way to describe it was that we all felt real again.

Third, we decided we needed to build events that used the Trojan horse concept—a massive push for proximity with no other agenda. And we had to start low-pressure relationships with people far from God. If you want to see a real-world example of this environment, go into any Barnes and Nobles bookstore:

Clerk: May I help you?
You: Why, yes, I would like to buy this book.
Clerk: Why? Just read it here.
You: Really?
Clerk: Sure. Grab a coffee and hit any one of our couches, or just lay in the aisle if you want.

Compare that to going to buy a car. A car salesman will hold on to your leg while you drag them off the lot. They cry, scream, and beg. They threaten and they beg some more. It's like all the hard parts of a ten-year relationship packed into fifteen minutes of sheer pressure. The difference is stark.

We tried to come up with a community event that everyone would like. It needed to be free and done well. In no time, we had all agreed that showing a movie outside in the evening would hold the best possibility for getting people together.

Who doesn't love a great movie? We bought some popcorn machines, a giant screen, and of course, another projector. This one was even more expensive than the others. It had to be bright enough to project while there was still some light in the sky.

Thankfully, there was a very generous family in our church who was pumped about this, and they had ample pesos to make it happen. You know people have money when they buy their groceries at the Sharper Image. They were—and still are—big players in our church, and many things we have done have happened because people like that came through financially. Mostly, I think they like rescuing us, so I keep putting us into harm's way so they can. It's a win-win-win for us, for them, and for God.

Back to the movies—we rented the local high school football field for six consecutive Friday nights in the summer, and we made signs that looked like giant director's slate clapboards saying "Free Movie Nights." In picking the movies, we wanted to get input from our entire church. They had good hearts, but it was evident from some of the suggestions that many were missing the point. The Chronicles of Narnia, The Passion of the Christ, and Fireproof were all big pushes. These are great Christian movies and all, but you think the average nonbeliever wants to go see these shows?

So the staff made an executive decision to pick more mainstream movies. Some had a few cuss words, and we didn't edit them. Everyone was on board with the picks—well, except for the Harry Potter movie. Several families got very upset that we were showing a movie they felt promoted magic and darkness. I listened to their concerns and tried to explain that I had seen the movie and felt it creatively illustrated the battle between good and evil.

Most came to an understanding, but one couple demanded another meeting to make their case. They said they would leave the church if we didn't change our stance. Sterling and I met with them over coffee. They said that we were "hurting God's Spirit" by showing something that showed magic, demons, and evil. Then the man said something that caused the coffee going down my throat to come shooting out of my nose. "Show something Christian, like Lord of the Rings."

Okay. I love Lord of the Rings just as much as the next guy, but anyone who has seen this trilogy has to admit that there are way scarier demons and a massive magic content. I asked them if they understood that these two movies are similar and have the same message about good and bad; they both involved magic and have dark creatures. They said that Tolkien was a Christian, so it was okay. We tried to talk it through, but in the end, they left the church. And we didn't show a Harry Potter movie. We showed two. They totally rocked. Those movies also opened the doors to many conversations about the struggle over light and darkness.

Over the last couple of years, our community has come to love our free movies—well, most people. You will always have someone upset with something you do. One group tried to get us kicked off the football field. Their argument was that it would disturb the elk and deer in the area; the animals use the field to feed on in the summer months. Obviously, they hadn't been to a football game there in a while. If they had, they would have seen that the field was Astroturf. Now, that must have really ticked off the elk! Think about being an elk and seeing all this green, luscious grass only to get a mouthful of rich, synthetic carpet. That's not cool.

But as a whole, we have seen hundreds upon hundreds of people come. We get to visit, hand out popcorn, and laugh with our neighbors and community. Many we only see a few times a year at movie nights. But we are friends now—and you can build on that. And yes, we have also seen it have an instant impact on the growth of our church. But in the end, we discovered the power of proximity. For our team, the fruit we saw from getting near people far from God is 90 percent of the battle.

Once we became neighbors and friends, we could be there to help our new friends if needed, whether it was with their kids, life problems, or to even share in their success and joy. And maybe—just maybe— someday we could invite them to meet the God that helped put our broken lives back together.

The success of our first Trojan horse event made us eager to build and launch more events and opportunities. We had tasted some success and got a real desire to get proximity with our community every day. But how? We were really hungry to matter, hungry to reach people … just plain hungry. And then someone had a thought that sent us crashing into our most successful growth engine to date.

"Hey, everyone has to eat, don't they?"

The Angry Llama

"Why does Sea World have a seafood restaurant? I'm halfway through my fish burger, and I realize, 'Oh my God ... I could be eating a slow learner.'"
-Lynda Montgomery

WHILE OUR MOVIE NIGHTS were a smashing success, some of our other outreach efforts were met with total failure. Our main push was to put a flyer on everyone's door in the community—something that told them we were there and wanted to be friends. This had worked for me at other churches, so we set off thinking it would be no different for us. We had no idea we were heading into a Steven King short story.

The first day, we headed out on foot. Six hours later, we had hit a staggering nine homes. We failed to understand how long the driveways are here and the fact that everyone lives about twenty-five acres apart. In the mountains of Colorado, if someone says, "Let's go to my neighbor's house," it usually involves a weather report and an Indian tracker. Lesson learned.

So we decided to overcome the hours of walking by purchasing four Go-Peds and using them to hit more homes. This was an instant hit with my very young and adventurous staff. Reaching people far from God with the help of the X Games was well received. For those of you who have never seen this device, a Go-Ped is a motorized skateboard with handlebars. They work well on flat surfaces but go pretty slow uphill. Nevertheless, we pressed on, and to our amazement, we began to tag more homes in an hour.

The next setback happened within the first week, and it was rather alarming—big dogs, loaded guns, and a few angry mountain people. We found that people in the mountains keep dogs more for protection than pets. We have our fair share of bears, elk, and mountain lions to deal with. Big dogs deal with them very well. For some reason, they also deal with twenty-two-year-old church-builders on Go-Peds just as effectively.

One of my guys, Adam, was the first and last to discover this. We were waiting in the van at the bottom of a driveway that had to be about half a mile. It was super-steep going up. As we watched him on the Go-Ped climbing slowly up the driveway, we noticed two small horses running to meet him. Then came the infamous words: "Wait! Those aren't horses! Those are dogs!" They did not look at all playful. They looked, in fact, testy. Look, I've been married for seventeen years now. I know what testy looks like, and they were carriers.

Unfortunately for Adam, he failed to see them when we did. We tried to call his cell but then realized that we had no cell service in the mountains. About the time he saw them, he had just enough time to turn around and get going—and did he go! Adam came down that hill at about 180 miles an hour. He weaved, moved, and jumped over holes! It was a thing of poetry, beauty, and grace.

And then suddenly, as he neared the van, his brakes failed. He jumped off the Go-Ped, rolled several times, and flew into the open doors of the van just in time for us to slam the door on Cujo and the Predator. The dogs took this in stride and began to attack our fifteen-passenger van instead. We laughed at them 'til it was clear they were actually making progress, and then we got out of there. We waited about a football field away until the dogs left, returned to get our Go-Ped, and then had an impromptu meeting to reevaluate our outreach strategy.

At the same time we were meeting the dogs, other staff members were meeting our heavily armed neighbors. As Brian was putting a flyer on a door, it swung open, revealing a very hairy man wearing only boxers and holding a shotgun. They were Tweety Bird boxers, to be very detailed. That holds no bearing on this story, but I find it hilarious.

Anyway, Tweety dude pointed the gun at Brian and asked, "What the hell are you doing on my land?!"

I felt that Brian's answer was very good considering the pressure he felt.

He summed it up in one word: "Leaving?"

The man pointed the gun at Brian till he got a

ways down the road, and then, to send the message home, the man fired a few rounds into the air. The message was received.

We got together later that day to recap—and of course, to let Brain and Adam change their pants. We laughed and retold the stories over and over. It was clear that this approach was not going to yield anything other than early funerals. So we went back to the drawing board. Cortland suggested a coffee shop. That way the community would come to us. This sounded great. I know a ton of churches that have had success at using coffee houses to bring people in. The only problem we saw was that the people up here did not look like the "chai latte, mocha cappuccino with soy milk" crowd. Add to that fact that just like every other place in America, there are 968 Starbucks cafes within a one-mile radius of each other. Brian suggested a bar. Brian is a Chicago native and very Irish. Every brainstorming session we have, Brian pushes to get the use of alcohol in. It's his passion. But in the end, we felt that people with that much firepower maybe needed less of the firewater.

That's when the idea of opening a full-service diner was born: an old-time diner and burger joint that served breakfast, lunch, and dinner. Conifer is actually about a forty-five-minute drive down to Denver. We call it "going down the hill." And that's where most people would go to eat out, since our town only has a few eateries.

We thought this was a good plan, so with less than $4,000, we rented a restaurant space (equipment included) and opened for business. Unfortunately, none of us knew anything about running a restaurant.

We served really stupid things the first two weeks like Pez and Pop Tarts. We deep-fried everything. At first, we did not charge our customers; we just wanted suggestions on how to make it better. We got a lot of great direction—comments like "close down now," "quit," and "kill your cook"—you know, constructive things like that. We realized that we needed the food to be good, or no one was going to come in. We needed better food. We tried looking online but had no Internet yet, due to spending all our money getting the place up and running.

So we drove down to Denver with our laptops and parked in the parking lot of a universally popular coffee shop. We would send one person in to buy the cheapest coffee item they had, and then they would get access to their Wi-Fi code. They would, in turn, text it to us in the van. Bam—we had all our laptops going.

We began to search the Food Network online and ultimately downloaded many episodes of Diners, Drive-ins, and Dives. We also got a lot from Throwdown with Bobby Flay. We took careful notes on how they made burgers, pulled pork sandwiches, and fries. We went to Sam's Club and spent literally the last $400 we had and re-opened the next day. And what do you know—it tasted good. Really good. Super-good. Well, not super-good, but pretty good.

Now all we needed was a name. That came in a conversation with a man who had just started attending our church. His name is Steve, and he has become a great friend and leader in the work here. He and his wife own a lot of animals. Some of them I understood, like chickens and cows. You can eat them. But he also had llamas. In fact, a lot of people up here have them.

I was joking about the herds I saw everywhere and how useless I thought they were. He educated me that day, informing me that a lot of ranchers who own sheep keep them around because llamas bond well with sheep. They are very protective animals. He began to tell me of stories where llamas have taken on bears in order to protect their friends. He said, "Michael, a llama will fight a grown mountain lion to protect its sheep. It will lose, but it will fight." I loved that line! Being in the shepherd business— so to speak—I was taken aback by the imagery. The Angry Llama Diner's name was born. It is the name that put us on the map here.

We then began signing up volunteers to serve in the diner every week. We have mechanics, lawyers, and computer programmers giving their time once or twice a week to work the grill or serve a table. The entire place runs on volunteers.

We don't hide the fact that it is a church-owned diner, but we never force any kind of God talk. In fact, it normally took the average customer two months before they knew the diner was run by a church. By then, it was too late. They liked us, and we liked them. If you walked in there right now, you couldn't tell it was an outreach tool. We are there to make friends—that's it!

However, as we did, many of our regulars have become part of our church. In fact, over 60 percent of our church members came as a direct result of The Angry Llama. They got curious and started asking questions. Next thing you know, we were having some awesome conversations about life, stress, raising kids, and hopelessness. For many in our community, that is the closest they want to get to God. We love them and have the opportunity to sit and talk with many of them for hours each week. We want them to know that they matter to us—whether they ever become a part of our church or not.

I have come to the realization that everyone has a church. Everyone belongs to a community. For some, it's a bar; for others, it's a gym or coffee shop. But we all turn to others. We crave connection. In our community, there is a feeling of isolation. Our diner helps those who are isolated—almost a thousand each week.

A few other benefits have come from The Angry Llama as well. Our church has four services each weekend in the same building as the diner. After the service, we give every new visitor a free family meal gift card. Many cash it in right away. The rest come back during the week. This gives us and our volunteers another chance to connect with them. It has been a raving success.

We also feed every local high school varsity sports team on their game days. Basketball, baseball, football, soccer, swimming, basket-weaving—we don't care. It's on us. Our desire is to engage with the local teens, and free food does this better than anything on earth.

After a few months, we even began to make a profit. The bulk of that goes into funding our rapidly growing youth ministry. But even when we started and were losing money like crazy, it was still worth it. I can't tell you how much of an impact it has had on our church. I think this is a killer idea that will really be a huge success in smaller communities.

I know a lot of churches have some type of food venue in their foyer. They are great, but in a small community, they can be the growth engine that shoots your church to the next level of impact. In the next three years, we have plans to launch a small general store and deli in a very isolated town up here. That community is miles from a supermarket, so we feel we can get proximity to them by selling staple groceries at a low cost. We will also start another Angry Llama diner in a larger city near us. We can't wait. We are addicted to connecting with others.

Even as I write this, I smile as I reflect back on all the failed attempts we had as a team trying to get even a conversation with people. I think of all the men, women, and kids who work hard to make the diner run so efficiently. And I think about the unbelievable young leaders God has brought to do all this.

I love my staff like family. We've had our moments—and still do, at times—but I could never do any of this without them. I feel like the days of the one-man show in church work is over. I think we would all do better if we built teams of friends and lived our whole lives together.

I also think of some wisdom I heard in a sermon by Bill Hybels: "Churches are built one ask at a time." Leadership teams are built one ask at a time. I remember when I started asking these guys to ditch their career plans and run off with me to build a church. I learned then and there the power of the ask. What can asking do?

This is the story of the Ask—duhn-duhn (Law and Order shout-out!).

How to Win Friends and Alienate Parents

"Life is never easy for those who dream."
-Robert Waller

JUST ONCE, I WOULD like to meet the person responsible for deciding what is sold in a Walgreen's store. I was there yesterday, and as always, it fascinated me. An older man in a cowboy hat was buying a five-pack of nail clippers, fifteen nine-volt batteries, two cases of beer, and a People magazine. What kind of party is this guy going to? Now, don't get me wrong, I love this store. In fact, after my last purchases, my wife had to do an intervention with me about what she calls my Walgreen's addiction.

"Sweetheart," she said, "the first step is to admit you have a problem."

I had been sent there to buy one Ace Bandage for my wounded son; I ended up buying over $60 worth of crap. Oh ... and I came home without the bandage. But the people who stock that store are geniuses. What pulls me in is that you never know what you'll see on the next aisle. Is it a Ginsu knife, a battery-powered cooler, or an umbrella hat? All of these seem like a good buy while I stand there talking myself into these purchases. It's eclecticism at its finest.

What I love about Walgreen's is exactly what I love about my staff. They have really no rhyme or reason to be doing ministry with me, but it is super-intriguing that God brought them. Over half of them never really planned to do church work until we all met. They come from all over the place: Vermont, Illinois, Kansas, Tennessee, Minnesota, Maryland, Texas, and Colorado.

They were a strange bunch when they got here. Both Joshes were filmmakers. Michelle was a nurse. Cortland was a pothead. Tiny and Melissa were professional ballet dancers. Adam was a snowboarder. Sterling was a struggling musician. Brian was an intellectual snob, and Justin was a true redneck. Emily came because she was into the struggling musician and said she was up for an adventure. My wife was and is a southern Texas girl through and through.

This was the core group that started the church. They sold their cars, worked like crazy, and began pushing this whole thing forward. And how did I get them to come with me to that level? I asked them. It's just that simple.

All my talks with them went something like this: "Hey have you ever thought about canceling your plans for the future and coming with me instead to build a church—not for a summer or even a year, but for the rest of your life?"

I was stunned at how many people said, "Sign me up."

I began to see that these guys and gals wanted significance more than success. They were in a hurry to make a difference to someone—to matter. I wished I would have known this truth years ago. For years, I tried to be a Swiss Army pastor. You know the type; we do it all: youth pastor, preacher, counselor, janitor, secretary, and lawn man. I was burning myself and my family out.

It reminded me of a trip I took overseas. Back in the day, I used to blow dry my hair. I know it's lame now, but understand that I was raised on the music of Bon Jovi and thus, I had to feather the 'fro. So anyway, I was at a hotel and wanted to plug in the dryer to sculpt my awesome locks and discovered that this crazy country put two round holes instead of a normal plug.

I took this in stride, because I'm an American. We overcome; we adapt. I happened to have a little tool kit in my luggage, so I used pliers to bend my straight prongs round. I then got it into the outlet and turned it on. That little dryer ran really fast for about four seconds … and then the entire room went black. Yeah, they use 220 instead of 110. Europeans, you crazy kids! Bye-bye, dryer.

That's exactly what my soul felt like after trying to run a church with little or no help. I decided that when I built this church, I would just ask for help and let the cards fall where they may. Now, please know that for every one team member who said yes, several said no. And even of those who said yes, a handful didn't stay. For many, the idea of living this adventure lost its appeal when it became work.

One young man's story comes to mind. He had worked with us for a little under five months. One night, he had coffee with a friend who was in town for a few days, and the very next morning, our young friend said he was quitting. It was sudden, but we all believe people have to do what their hearts tell them. We asked what brought on the sudden change. He said that as he told this friend all about how we live and do ministry, his friend kept saying, "That's epic! That's awesome!"

His friend began to tell him how he was jealous about this life and wanted to live the same way. Our pal then said that after he got home, he realized that living this epic of a Christian life was more work than he wanted. He said it sounds great to talk about until you have to wake up at 6:00 a.m. every day— until you have to give the last of your money to help a family buy food. Until you have to share a one-bedroom apartment for two years with four other guys. He said, "I lived it, and honestly, the reality of it is not nearly as fun as the idea of it." And there you have it.

There is a massive difference between ministry in theory and ministry in actuality. Even to this day, people who come to work with us see quickly the amount of work it takes to do this. Recently, we have had interns ask to come work with us and learn how we do church. Some can't even work one week without getting irked that we don't do more "real" ministry. They think that running the diner, showing movies outdoors to hundreds, or cutting wood to heat homes for those who can't afford wood is nothing more than menial labor. Sure, they say things like, "I know that's important too, but …" They want to counsel, lead Bible studies, or run prayer groups.

Many think that ministry is only about getting up on Sundays and preaching, leading worship, or having a cool title. And while I understand their desires, I can't help but to be saddened by the mindset they refuse to give up. We try to challenge them to look at every job in the church the way Christ says to look at them: everything we do for the kingdom needs to be done with a real zeal and passion. Some take this challenge, grow, and they begin to be real, mature leaders. But for those who don't, we realize they are kids in their early twenties who believe they know best. We pull back and let them attend only the things they think are real ministry, and those fade away pretty quickly. They get their way, but they miss out on things that would benefit them a great deal. We have come to realize that God has to teach them lessons that they refuse to learn from us.

One of the defining qualities of my team is that they never backed down from hard work and chose to see that everything they put their hands to do could be leveraged by God to reach or care for people. They kept showing up every day with their big boy pants on and worked through relationships and hurts and slowly became a family. And a family is exactly what we are now. Our culture has had a drastic shift in what we think a family is. You can clearly see this cultural paradigm shift in even our TV programs.

Years ago, people watched Happy Days, The Cosby Show, Growing Pains, and Family Ties. All the while, our families were self-destructing at an alarming rate, but built inside us all is the absolute need for a family. We all begin to make them from the people we find along the way. Popular shows began to reflect this, and we dialed in, because it made sense to most of us. Shows like Friends, Seinfeld, How I Met Your Mother, and Sex in the City began to take over, because most of us could not relate to a real family anymore, but we had a family of friends.

Of the thirteen of us who started this church, only four did not come from a broken home. And as weird as it sounds, I believe God used that to knit us together in a way that makes us tough to rip apart. People can leave co-workers and relatives, but when you spend years caring for each other through sicknesses and life's trials—when the entire staff sits in a hospital waiting for the birth of the next little baby—it changes you. You find yourself loving your life; you begin to see that the Bible was right when it says God sets the solitary in families. You feel safe and realize that you are now home. It's hard to walk away from that.

I spent my life wishing my dad would have wanted me. I wished he would have shown up at a football game or sent a letter. He never did. I looked for other men to fill that gap as well, but it never happened. Instead, God surrounded me with true brothers and sisters. We want to do our whole lives together. We used to joke that if the church fell apart, we would start some business and all live in the same neighborhood. It's not a joke anymore—we would.

We need that level of love and commitment from the core leaders. We reproduce what we are. If your staff is divided and clique-ish, don't be surprised if your church becomes the same way. My kids look, act, and talk like me and my wife. Why? Because they are raised in the world my wife and I show them. The same is true of our teams. We need to be close and bond.

I believe this is one of the senior leader's most important jobs. For years, I was the only paycheck these guys got. I had to learn to praise them more and love them. That included hugging them, which was hard, because I ain't a touchy-feely kind of guy. I also began to try to break up the monotony of the weeks and months by bringing fun into their lives.

From time to time, I run through the church offices and try to shoot my staff with paintball guns. We play Wii tennis, ping-pong, and will even close everything down to go to a movie. We have random contests for money. We make paper airplanes and whoever's stays in the air longest wins $50. Sometimes we play Texas Hold 'Em during office hours, take personality tests, and sock wrestle. That last one is tough to explain. Every Easter week, we have a team contest to see how many Peeps one person can eat in ten minutes. Brian won last year with 127 ... then his spleen exploded.

I cannot stress how much I feel responsible to make the lives of my staff members fun. In all areas of church work, we traffic in the hurts and problems of others. It can wear out the most zealous Christian leader. Most of you reading this know what I'm talking about. So in order to stay balanced, we have raucous fun, too.

It falls on me to bring the thunder each week. It bonds us, and when the enemy comes to divide us, he has a really hard time. I mean it. To this day, I have never had a team member quit that I have shot with paintballs. I have not seen an official study on this, but I am batting a thousand on this one, so I'll keep it up.

One quick note of warning about asking before we move on: When I began to ask these very young guys and gals to come build a church with me, it didn't go over well with several of their parents or family members. Be ready for that backlash. Even though they were all adults, some of their parents were leery of them working for God. One dad asked his son, "Well, does God cover dental?" Several called me and expressed intense disapproval. I tried talking to the ones who were Christians, but in the end, they stayed angry for a while. Only time and success have changed things. Now our biggest critics have become our biggest fans. It's funny how success validates every leadership style or plan. I really don't have any advice on this except to say that if it happens, know that it passes. Stay strong.

The conclusion I have come to is that God will bring the right people for your team close enough to talk to, and then it's in your court to ask them to join up. Jesus was the greatest example of this. He would walk up to future leaders and say, "Hey, leave your career plans, and let's go rock the world together." Many got up, put their plans and careers down, and went off to change the world. We all know friends and acquaintances who might sign up for a life change if someone would just ask them. Many are even longing for it. Yes, some will say no, so what's the harm? But when some say yes (and some will), you will all begin to become a bigger threat to darkness.

Being together and being friends is over half the battle, but there are still things we are learning every day. We want to keep growing in Christ and as leaders. We received an education on many things over these few years. Some lessons we learned from books, podcasts, and wise counsel; others we learned the hard way—and we have the scars to prove it. Most of our education was on what to do well and what would profit us as a church team and Christ-followers. But it was by accident that we found a few things we will not forget. We learned about three things that never, ever profit a leader.

Flying Monkeys Suck

"When I hit a problem in the youth group, I fix it by asking myself just one simple question: what would Jack Bauer do?"
-Cortland Coffey, The Journey Youth Pastor

MY TEENAGE SON HAS a shirt that reads, "It's all fun and games till the flying monkeys show up." This is, of course, referring to the movie The Wizard of Oz. I can remember years ago when it aired on primetime television uninterrupted. My son, Titus, was about four at the time, and I thought watching it would be a fun family thing to do. It had been years and years since I last saw this movie, so we made popcorn and settled in for some Cheshire family bonding.

The movie started out fine. Titus was a little bothered when a house fell on a person, and the Wicked Witch was not well received, but other than that, he seemed fine—that is, until the part where those monkeys come flying in from all over the sky and wreak havoc on this unlikely group of friends. He was very upset about it. I had to turn it off and tell him the rest of the story so he would know that the monkeys didn't win in the end.

I would love to say he got over it right away, but weeks later, we went to the local zoo, and when he saw the monkeys, he had a flashback. After I pointed out that these caged furry animals had no wings, he was cool with it, but he preferred to quickly move on. Even years later, he's still just not into monkeys. What can I say? I scarred him.

Truth be told, I have had to deal with some flying monkeys in my life of ministry as well—issues that come in unannounced and begin to cause all kinds of problems with my soul. They bring only pain and frustration and leave only regrets. For me and my team, we have an inside joke about three problems we call "flying monkeys." If one of us starts to struggle with one of these, another team member will inevitably say, "Hey, you got a monkey flying in" or "There's a monkey on your back." We do it in jest, but with the idea of letting the other person know we see them heading down a bad road.

To be a Christian leader means that we will all dance with these three things many times in the course of our lives. Please understand that all three will never profit you anything. The longer they are even entertained, the stronger they will grow, leaving us with a broken conscience. I firmly believe that God has given us a conscience as a compass. It guides and directs our choices and feelings. But the Word of God clearly says that the conscience can get defiled and even seared. It can give false readings that can be very dangerous for any person in leadership. We need a correct, sharp reading.

When I get on a plane to fly to another state, I know the pilots are using a compass that is very precise. If I thought they were using one found in a Cracker Jack box, I would exit the plane immediately. Sure, it may point in generally the right direction, but the more miles you add to the trip, the further off course you get, even if you're off by one degree. I need precision in air travel. Our lives depend on it. This is also very true for the conscience of a church leader. We need a true reading, or we can make decisions based on false feelings or bad attitudes. I have three things to share with you that I have had to guard against coming into my own life and heart.

First is unforgiveness. Yes, I know that we all know this. But wait—it is still a massive temptation for us all. The truth is that no one warned me how many shots you take as a church leader. Many times, unforgiveness seems like it protects me from feeling used. In the earliest months of our ministry, we had a young family in our church go through a massive upheaval in their relationship. It involved law enforcement and a real damage in trust. A divorce seemed inevitable. We had to help with bills and rent, find the man a separate place to stay, and spend hundreds of hours counseling in an attempt to patch up hurt feelings. It was truly hard on our emotions and our finances.

Over time, things began to heal, and the couple reconciled. No sooner had that happened than they stopped coming around. We pressed in, called, e-mailed, and asked to talk. After weeks of pursuing them, they sent a letter thanking us for helping, but they wanted a new church where no one knew their problems. They thanked us for everything we did. Now that they were fixed, they wanted to start over with people who had no idea of their struggles.

This was a hurtful thing for my young staff. They spent a lot of time loving and caring for the family. They gave up their own money to help this couple and even babysat their kids from time to time. And just when things were getting better, we were brushed off. Over the next few weeks, it seemed as though we were all fine.

Then one evening, we got a call from a different couple in our church who needed similar help. The next morning, we talked about it for a couple hours. The general feeling was to stay hands-off. We had never been the hands-off kind of people. Slowly, we realized that we were mad about how we were kicked to the curb by those we loved and helped. We had to really forgive them or we would never be able to see each situation clearly. And we did.

Over the years, we have had to forgive and let go of many other instances where we felt misjudged or used. We know that we have to have an open heart for the next person or family that needs help. In ministry, we have to keep the understanding that hurt people will hurt people. Many times it's those we care for most.

While I was being trained for ministry, I spent several years as a fire fighter. One day on and two days off was my schedule, which gave me the opportunity to work around the church I attended. Now, while I loved the excitement of being a firefighter, the only part that I didn't like was all the medical calls we went on. In fact, most calls were of a medical nature. We went to many fights, mishaps, and car accidents.

Many times, on scene, I would start to help a victim, and they would fight and kick at me. No hurt person ever handed me their broken arm; they held it close to their body and would protect it from my touch. Many times they would say uncool things about my mother's ancestry or use un-churchy words. But even though they threw fits and said vile things, we never left them there. We never got mad at them or thought they were bad people. They were hurt, and we could clearly see it.

Unfortunately, it's much harder to see the hurts in people's hearts—but those hurts can make them just as mean. Over time, we all have learned to recognize that anyone who lashes out at us or chooses to walk out of our lives has hurts, and we understand that pain makes us all act differently than who we really are. So we guard ourselves and each other from being unforgiving toward anyone.

The second thing that never profits you in ministry is fear. Don't kid yourself; fear follows us our whole life looking for a way in. We can fear failure, fear other people, fear success, fear misunderstandings, fear gossip, and fear the Board of Elders. Fear is the greatest shape shifter you will ever meet. It comes in as caution or discernment. It comes through friends, e-mails, or phone calls. And fear will never ever help any of us in our pursuit of God's calling. It's funny; I would not ever classify myself as a fearful person. I've been a firefighter, worked as a bouncer, and have been in more than my share of fights. I'm okay with pain, and I believe it's not tragic to die if you're standing up for what's right. But the fear in church work is way more subtle than that.

I can still recall being at a conference for church leaders years ago. A leader was talking about the nightmare he went through by not standing up against a big giver who was using his checkbook to push his agenda. I remember thinking that I would never be tempted to give into those kinds of people. At that time, the biggest giver in my church was dropping about $100 a month, and she was my wife. I filed that away for things that weaker leaders needed to know, and I kept on trucking forward in ministry. Wouldn't you know—over time, God brought some pretty wealthy people to my church.

A certain man used to drop about two thousand a week into the offering. For many churches this may not seem like a lot, but for my church of a little over two hundred, it was huge! He was—and is—a very nice man, but he had ideas about where we should use his money. He would hint at buying this or that.

One thing he really wanted us to buy was a new church van. I told him our old one was just fine, but he wouldn't drop it. Then one afternoon, he showed up with a shiny new van. "Here you go, kid." He tossed the keys to me. I, of course, said thanks and that he was crazy. Awesome. But in the back of my mind, I wondered if he would stop giving for a while because he bought this. He did.

He began to show up every few weeks with a new this or that. He was deciding what the church needed and was overriding everyone else because he could. I knew I needed to talk to him about it … and that is when I met fear. What if he got offended and left? What if he was right and we should have bought those things? I spent two long days debating this and then picked up the phone to set up a meeting for later that afternoon.

I loaded all the stuff he had bought into that new van and took it to the restaurant where we were to meet. He was already eating when I arrived. I sat down, ordered coffee, and slid the keys to the van across the table. I said, "I want you to know that I love your giving spirit and could really use your support, but I can't let you hijack my budget anymore. I don't want you to put the money to what you want. We have a youth group who needs funding, single moms who need help with their rent, and other needs that a fifteen-passenger van can't help."

I asked him to either give with no strings attached or give somewhere else.   I said my piece and waited for the backlash. He wiped his face and said, "Michael, that took guts. I have never heard anyone say it that way. I love that phrase—'hijacking the budget.' I'm truly sorry. Please forgive me. I didn't see the whole picture." He said to keep or sell the van and equipment and that the next Sunday, he would catch us up on our budget downfalls. And he did. It was a God moment in my life.

But not all my stories like this end well. Several times, I have slid checks across the table to people who demanded their way only to have them snatch up their check, say "fine," and walk off. But each and every time, God came through. Fear accompanies me to each meeting, but the minute I open my mouth and address the concern, it disappears. No matter what the outcome, fear loses every time. Of course, this is only one example of fear, but in every case, it comes to dissuade us from making the right call in the leadership of our churches and ministries.

And now for the final point and my personal

favorite—self-pity. Self-pity has the ability to make your worst nightmares come true. It gives false permission to sin; it causes you to hate or quit. To indulge in self-pity is to choose to be a victim in life. I have a framed quote in my office by D. H. Lawrence that says, "I have never seen a wild thing sorry for itself. A small bird will fall frozen from a bough without ever feeling sorry for itself." Wow! I love it! I can feel God all over it! If we are to change this dark world, then we must never get pulled into the self-pity game.

I had a special lady who was my spiritual mother. She used to tell me things like, "Michael, life sucks, so wear a helmet." She knew that if I was going to make it in church work, then I had to be able to take a hit without turning it into some sad story. When we drift into self-pity, the very tools we need as leaders begin to lose power: vision, purpose, passion, and a sense of calling give way to apathy and disappear. "Look, if you want to do anything of significance, you need resistance." Everyone gets resisted. God has Satan, Superman had Lex Luthor, and Gilligan had that island. You have ... well, someone.

You're not being attacked; you're being resisted. In your church, ministry, or city, you are the invading army. We have come for our communities, so we should expect to be in the line of fire. It's all good. As Winston Churchill said, "There is nothing more exhilarating in life than to be shot at with no effect." Don't get caught up in feeling like you're the only one. God called you and put a fighting spirit in you. Let it out. We are in the people business, and it's a brutal business at that. You are equal to the task if you refuse to feel sorry for yourself. Make no excuses! Let's play like champions!

Okay. That's enough time spent on the soap box for a while. Back to the story.

As our church began to grow faster and faster, the economy kept falling to new lows, and as that happened, many in our church and community began to find less income to handle life's unexpected problems. We needed to find a way to meet these needs faster. We needed to really get things moving. We needed to get fast and furious—and right away!

The Flux Capacitor

"Shake and bake!"
-Ricky Bobby, Talladega Nights

I KNOW NOTHING ABOUT cars. Sure, I know that Pistons are a pro basketball team in Detroit, that the British accent on my Garmin makes my car feel classy, and that if your turn signal doesn't work, you should check your blinker fluid. Other than that, I'm lost. So when a few men in our congregation asked if our church could build a race car, I was confused.

"What kind of racing?"

Drag racing. They explained that in Denver, we have a very high-profile drag racing stadium. Bandimere Speedway is open to the public each Wednesday night for anyone to race a car.

Now, the man in me instantly lurched forward and said "Yes!" while the church leader in me said "Why?" The conversation pressed on. The pitch was that by building a race car, men who would never walk in the church doors might come to be part of this car-building process. "It gives us proximity to them" was their selling point. These men obviously had never slept through a sermon, as my words were coming back to bite me in the butt.

They also thought it would be a good way to get the youth involved as well; Bandimere sponsors special youth nights at the track. Honestly, the idea of using it to get near people who normally would not come to church excited me. Up here, we are always looking for opportunities to get our youth active and doing something.

My only hangup was what the cost might be. I told them that I couldn't justify putting our very limited money into a race car when there were real needs that had to be met.

"It could pay for itself from crushed cars."

Okay, they had my attention. What is a crushed car? They went on to tell me that when a car is dead, you can take it to a crushing yard. Cash is given according to the weight of the car. One can pocket anywhere between three hundred and five hundred dollars. I asked my mechanic friend where we would get all these cars no one wanted. The answer was obvious: front yards.

With the donation of the body of a 1968 Cornet, men began to build a drag racing car. The first engine came out of a junked mobile home. They had to cut out the entire side of the camper to retrieve the engine. It was awesome. They did body work and installed the engine—and boy, was it loud. We were literally off to the races!

Both men and woman from our church and community got a chance to drive it. Even my wife took a turn. She did very well, but this came as no surprise to me, as I have ridden shotgun with her for almost twenty years. She has condensed driving down to two simple actions: pedal to the floor and slamming on the brakes. She often does the driving so the kids and I have many an opportunity to grow in our prayer life. But in a race car, she is in her world. Over that first year, our car progressively got better, and by the end of the season, we actually won a trophy. That's right. We took home the hardware.

Now although we started this to help reach people in our community, the race team and its core leaders began to see some other benefits grow out of this idea. For one, we saw it connect people in our church who normally would not get to know each other. You could have a fifty-eight-year-old bearded lumberjack hanging out with the awkward twenty-three-year-old computer programmer. When people in our churches start becoming friends with those outside of church, everybody wins.

Another great find came about from our struggling economy. Like so many churches, we have seen our fair share of people losing their jobs, houses, and cars. We actually started this church at the same time the economy began to tank. Instantly, people began to turn to us for help.

Many times, we can solve home or health care problems with social programs, but car repairs only get fixed with cash. When a family had a car in need of repair that was just too costly, we would try to scrounge up cash to get it fixed. This also meant we were at the mercy of mechanics who may not be completely honest with us.

"Yes sir, you're going to need a new drive shaft."

"Really?"

"Yes. It seems like your old one is growing resentful of the rest of your car and pulling away."

"How much is that going to cost?"

"Normally, it's $1200, but I can get a rebuilt one for $1199.99. You know, because I like you."

Conversations like this got old.

So our mechanics began to fix the car issues people were having; the church only had to foot the bill for parts. Each Monday night, these greasy heroes would repair vehicles for single moms or give the church van yet another tune-up or oil change. They began to work more on other cars than the race car. It was a wonderful thing to see the church take care of its own. As the word spread about this ministry, some in our church began to use it to leverage a better relationship with friends they were trying to win to Christ.

One morning, a teacher in our church called and asked if our auto guys could help a friend and co-worker. She said that her fellow teacher was on the way to school when the back tire just fell off. We assured her we would look into it. Upon investigation, every lug nut and stem had snapped off. I thought the car was a goner. But the guys took it to the shop, and within two hours, they had it fixed. Not only had they fixed it, but they changed the oil, repaired a broken door, filled it with gas, and cleaned it inside and out. We delivered it to her school with a note that read, "You matter to God. You matter to us." How can we tell people that God cares for them and loves them when it seems like God doesn't even care if their car breaks down? Stories like that have helped us open doors to hearts that have been shut for years.

One really cool thing I love about this ministry is that the idea and leadership has come from a man who is not on our church staff. Doug is the fleet manager at the Platte Canyon Fire Protection District, he works a physically demanding full-time job and has a family; yet somehow, he makes time to care for many others. On some nights, when almost no other volunteers show up, this guy stays and puts in hours fixing broken-down cars and trucks that sideline families. I can't tell you how valuable people like that are. In a world of "me, me, me," they sweat and serve people who could never afford to pay them. I asked Doug one day why he did it.

"Because I can and you can't, Mike." Doug's mantra was, "Call me. Don't try to fix it; call me."

In many ways, these mechanics have a grasp on ministry that even some pastors don't. They know what they are good at and leverage it to impact lives. It is a true statement to say that because of their willingness to restore cars to a working condition, they have also restored some people's belief in a loving God. May their tribes increase!

We have not stopped learning from our racing team ministry; the lessons keep coming with regularity. In the end, we love trying new things—anything that gets us near our community to become friends. We had reached out to the hungry, the moviegoers, and the mechanically challenged, but we were still not getting near our teens at the rate in which we wanted.

Our community has had its fair share of tragic youth stories. But teens are a tough crowd to gain acceptance with, especially for church leaders … and then a woman in our church had a great idea that we are fixing to launch. What does every teenager want? Freedom. And what do they need to get it? A car. What do you need to drive? A license! Yahtzee!

Ten and Two

Student drivers—Father, forgive them; they know not where they go!

Y EARS AGO, BEFORE I was even married, I went on a mission trip to a far-off land. I had some pals who had been there the year before, and they warned me that I would find the food less than appealing. So, not wanting to go hungry, I paid a visit to my neighborhood Wal-Mart the night before I left to grab some snacks. You know, cheese crackers, trail mix, and gum. On my way out of the store, I passed a display of Pringles that were on sale for an astounding eighty-nine cents a can! Wow! I took twelve. Food issue—over! I packed them carefully in my suitcase.

After the sixteen-hour flight, we claimed our luggage and spent another four hours in a van weaving our way to a remote little village. When we arrived, we were escorted to our room, and I immediately began to unpack. Now, I'm not sure what caused such disarray and chaos—maybe the pressure in the luggage compartment was different from where I sat—but all twelve Pringles cans had exploded. Every single chip had been reduced to crumbs, and these crumbs found their way into each fold, crease, and pocket in my clothes. I spent an hour shaking them out and wiping out my bag. Of course, you could see the tiny grease stains of deliciousness on every inch of my wardrobe, and I smelled of one giant Pringle.

It only took me one day to realize that my friends were wrong about the local cuisine. It's not that it was unappealing, it was just plain inedible! Every time I sat down to eat, it was like I was in a scene in Indiana Jones and the Temple of Doom. These foreigners ate stuff that Fear Factor wouldn't even dare one to eat. Now, I know what many of you Christians will say. "Oh, you have to eat it, or you'll offend them." Whatever. The Bible says that it is harder to win an offended brother than to take a walled city. I'll take the challenge—I'm a pretty good climber—but there was no way I was going to eat some of their "delicacies." "I'm sorry. I have an allergy that flares up every time I eat monkey balls. I'll have to pass. Too bad, too. They look good."

Anyway, back to the Pringles. For the entire two weeks I was there, I smelled like those chips. And every time I went anywhere, I had local teenage kids follow me, smelling and licking my shirts. They sought me out like I was a tasty rock star. Even my fellow American travelers would fight to sit next to me so they could get a whiff of that salty, greasy anointing. That was the only time in my life I found it easy to attract teenagers as a church worker. The rest of the time, it is tough to get near them. That toughness is no different up here in the Rockies.

Our community offers very little to entertain our kids. We have no theaters, bowling alleys, miniature golf, malls, or music venues. There are no cool and trendy coffee shops targeting youth, and in our city, we have no rec center. So what are teens to do? Good question. For quite a few of them, the answer is pot.

If you circle the parking lot of our local supermarket every Friday and Saturday night, you can find a brood of kids hanging out on the hoods of their cars with music blaring and doobies lit. Some find a driver and head off to Denver in search of entertainment while others just veg out in front of their TV. Sure, there are some awesome parents who work very hard to get their kids involved in activities, but for every parent like that, you have another parent who has too many life issues of his or her own to help get the kids moving.

We believe that the church can play a critical role in guiding young people toward a rewarding life and purpose if we can just get near them. A woman in our church brought the idea of us starting a driving school. The logic is simple: every kid wants to drive. To do so, every kid is required to take driver's ed. What if four of our youth pastors got state certified to teach this class and we began to offer it to kids at a very low price? The average driving school costs between $350 and $400 to complete the course. We could do it all for no more than $200. We could even give scholarships away for those who cannot afford it.

We also are working hard to make it fun,

educational, and interesting for them. Now, while we will never use this to talk about God, every student will know that a church sponsors this school and that all the trainers are also youth pastors. My theory is that after spending thirty hours being taught by Cortland, Sterling, Adam, or Melissa, these kids will bond enough with them that they might call them if ever they hit a hard patch in life. Again, we want to be friends first, and if asked, we can talk about God. If not, we are still pals.

We are also trying to serve the parents as well. Some parents in our church said that taking their kids to driver's ed was awful because they had to wait for the kids for hours in their car. Many people live too far away from the nearest driving school; the trip to and from—times two—is just too much. We are committing to feed every student and their chaperone at our diner. We hope that this gives us additional insight into the families we long to help in our community.

Even as I write this, we are getting ramped up, and with so many details still needing to be ironed out, the idea of whether it will even work is still up in the air. But no matter what, we will try. I have a pretty good feeling about it, honestly. I only share it with you because I'm stoked about the possible doors this could open.

If you do nothing, then that is exactly what you get. If you try some new things, then every once in a while, you knock it out of the park. I feel this will be one of those game-changing ideas. Ideas that help you get to people whom you wouldn't otherwise get to are always in demand. I believe to the core of my being that every person has thoughts of God at some point in his or her life.

There are doorways that open for a time, and if we are close enough, we can be the ones to point people toward God. Those doors open up most when people are hurt or in need. It's in these times that the church can find itself in its finest hour—that is, if it can meet the needs of the hurting—if it can be strong, wise, and courageous. The church that partners with the hurt, fights for the downcast, and loves the broken will win. It's that simple.

I See Dead People

"Even the strongest have their moments of fatigue."

-Friedrich Nietzsche

WHEN DID THIS BECOME okay?" I asked that question to a middle-aged woman while sitting on the plywood floor of a shed in the parking lot of a home improvement store.

The store had several sheds set up for display. You could go in and check them out anytime. Little did the employees know that during the late night hours, a couple would make the long drive to meet there and use it to shelter their illicit relationship.

I was called there in the early morning hours because the man she was so willing to lose her family to had just informed her he wanted to stop; he loved his wife. This revelation came after he had used her just one more time. The conversation boiled into an argument, and when she threatened to go tell the wife everything, he put on his clothes, gathered hers as well, and left her in that shed alone, naked, and ashamed. Classy guy!

She crept to her car and got her phone. She tried calling some friends, but no one answered. Finally, after a few hours, she gathered her courage and called her pastor. "I need help. Please come alone and bring a blanket." When I got there, I covered her up, and we talked for over an hour. We took that moment of extreme hurt to understand how she ended up there. We prayed, we even laughed, and then I followed her home and made sure she pulled into her garage and closed the door. It took a while—a lot of tears and counseling—but in the end, her heart healed; her own marriage was fixed as she began to live a different life.

And that, ladies and gentleman, is what all of us in church work signed up for. We take people's nightmares and work to get them to the God of their dreams. Not all stories have happy endings, and not every person wants help, but we are, nonetheless, called to put ourselves into harm's way and care.

When I was just training to be a pastor, I would get excited about the opportunity to do some real, hands-on ministry with broken people. I had no idea how many broken people there actually were. Many, who I saw every day and thought had no problems, would suddenly and without warning self-destruct. It was also a blow to my spirit when I came to realize that I couldn't help everyone—that some people choose the wrong path even after the warning shots of God have flown over their heads.

The temptation in my early years was to pull back. I'd just pray for people and do my sermons, but I couldn't really fix anything, so why try? This was not the best attitude, I admit. The Scripture that always set me back on track is in the first chapter of James. James talked about faith and works. James said, what good are you to people if they say, "I'm cold, and I'm hungry," and you say, "Go! Be warm and be filled!"? What good are we if all we do is say a prayer for people? Where are the power, love, and sacrifice in that?

I've talked to quite a few leaders who have backed off from helping—not because they are unloving, but rather because they feel overwhelmed that there are so many needs. I understand the feeling, but also feel that in doing so, we are missing the best opportunity to penetrate hearts. And after all, is that not our goal?

You have already read that money was scarce in the beginning of this church plant. So when problems came to our attention, we had very little cash to help anyone. Add to that the very true words of Shakespeare, who said that when troubles come, they come not as single spies but as battalions: people losing their jobs, behind on their mortgage or rent, with broken down-cars and all other types of money issues. And then there's the growing number of people who cannot afford health care but make a little too much to get help from the government.

Out of the gate, we were hit with all these issues and more. And to be honest, we would have been overwhelmed if it had not been for a handful of very young and driven staffers who believed they could find a way to help anyone. This department was led by a young woman named Melissa who began to learn about every state, federal, and city program for every imaginable issue that could arise. Melissa and her team began to assist people in getting health care and food stamps.

This caused some disagreements with a few Christians in our church who felt we should not point people to government programs. They quoted their favorite radio talk show personalities and preachers when explaining that we would be creating dependents. It was the same old argument I had heard before; we were creating dependents that everyone would have to pay for with their tax money.

I tried to listen calmly and be rational in my alternate opinions, but I must admit that the level of selfishness began to irk me. At what point did Jesus just get ticked off and start spin kicking people in the temple? Can I do that? After all, I have the WWJD bracelet. Can we just follow Christ and his book and let everyone with a TV news or radio show have opinions and not the final truth? Just because a famous personality has the same opinion as me about abortion does not mean that I'm drinking all the Kool-Aid they are serving.

We are supposed to help the hurt. So some use us—it's fine. Jesus healed arms that might steal someday. He healed legs that would carry these people to sin and eyes that could be used to covet and lust ... but he healed them anyway. And if you get used by some, then remember it, learn from it, and grow wiser next time, but let's keep trying! Okay. Sorry, my tiny rant is over.

And now back to our story. With so many people in our community losing their jobs due to downsizing and such, we made it our business to help them find jobs. We surfed Craigslist, classifieds, and local

Manpower services. We taught men and women how to look for a job and showed them which ones were scams. Slowly, we began to find work for some. We networked between business owners in our church and those in need of employment. This worked as well.

At this same time, many families were coming to the conclusion that they needed to downsize. They needed a smaller house or to sell a car. Again, Melissa's team began helping to post homes and vehicles for sale on the internet along with searching for cheaper places to live. Even in this economy, Melissa's team was able to assist four of six homes to sell in the last twelve months just by getting that information on every website they could find.

Our goal was to come alongside our church and community and be God-centered social workers, cheerleaders, researchers, prayer partners, counselors, and advocates. We may not have all the answers, but we can find them with God's help and Google. We decided that Christ would never bring us a problem that we couldn't get his wisdom on and help with. In this process, we have come to the end of our ideas several times—and then, wouldn't you know it, God takes over. And FYI, he is really good at sorting things out in record time.

We have learned that some people need to work with us to solve their own problems and that if they refuse, then we will wait on them before doing it for them. We work to get the right people in the room, the coffee in us, and the brains storming. And I must say that it feels good to make a difference. It's almost an addiction to help some take a hill that they haven't been able to conquer on their own. I guess God got it right when he said we are stronger together than we are apart.

I often think back to the day I visited that woman in the shed. I think of how we all—in some way, shape, or form—end up in a moment when we ask ourselves, "When did things get so far off track?" The reality is that pain and mistakes will forever be part of the human race on this side of heaven, and because of that, we will continue to have open doors to human hearts—job security, if you will. We just have to be willing to get neck-deep in others' messes. We have to heal the hurt, comfort the broken, and give an answer to even the toughest of questions—questions like:

"Where is God when I hurt?"

"Why did my dad leave?"

And of course, the one question that has plagued mankind for the ages …

Why Do Men Have Nipples?

"I know God will not give me more than I can handle. I just wish He didn't trust me so much."

-Mother Teresa

RECENTLY, MY WIFE AND I went with several of our staff members to swim with the sharks at the local Denver aquarium. You get to put on wetsuits and snorkel in a tank full of fish including three or four nurse sharks that quite honestly never move. I'm not sure, but I think they were high. I need more testing to be sure. Anyway, before we got in, the instructor gave us the drill about not trying to touch the animals but just observing them. He said many of them were pretty old and pointed out a very large sea turtle as one of the senior members in the water.

With the necessary info in hand, we entered the water. I was in for only about two minutes when I felt someone touching my butt inappropriately. I looked back, thinking I would see my wife. That woman can't keep her hands off me. I don't blame her. I have a mirror; I've seen the goods. But what do you know; it was the giant sea turtle. He wanted to play.

The instructor came over and asked me to try not to interact with him. I assured him I was not looking to get probed by the turtle and the whole thing had gotten me shell-shocked as well. He didn't laugh, but I thought I was pretty witty. Anyway, I kept swimming, and the turtle kept following me. No matter where I went, he was constantly making moves on me. Even the instructor began to laugh and said that he had never seen the turtle act that way.

When it was time to get out, we sat in a shallow pool taking off our gear while the turtle floated next to me with his big, sad eyes. I tried to tell him that this relationship was doomed from the start. "I'm an extrovert, and you live your life hidden in a shell. We are just too unequally yoked." No matter what I said, nothing seemed to comfort him, so I stroked his shell one last time, and we went our separate ways. The last thing I saw was those big, friendly eyes watching his friend walk out of his life forever.

That day, the turtle had the exact look on his face that seekers get when you have to answer some hard questions about God. It's really one of the worst parts of ministry. Some people come seeking and walk away having found Christ, but there are always a few who hit a deal breaker, and you can see that a relationship with Christ may not happen at that moment—or maybe ever.

Overall, I love being a Christian, but even coming into the faith, there are some issues and stances I wish I could change. Many times, we have to have tough conversations about issues that no one wants to touch but we are forced to deal with.

One of my first encounters with this was on the topic of gays. In this day and age, many (if not all) families have a member that struggles with this. These people are loved and cared for by those close to them but want to know why God hates them. They get their ideas of God's hate for gays from many churches and religious leaders who stand up and speak for all of us.

Add to that my personal friendships with several gay men. I consider many to be close friends. They have stayed in my home and spent time with my family. They are kind, good people whom I would fly across the world to help. I firmly believe that God loves them as much as you or me. But I still cannot change what His Word says. I cannot change what the Bible says about that lifestyle.

Now, if you ever come to any church I preach in, you will never hear me rail against gay people or tell them to leave. There are several who attend our church weekly and are investigating the faith. I won't kick out gays, because then I have to kick out the liars, adulterers, thieves, and gossips. Just that last group leaving would turn most of our churches into ghost towns. I believe it's wrong—not because I'm not gay, but because the Bible clearly says it's wrong. I have studied other denominations that have overturned this, but in the end, I couldn't find any other way around it without changing the Word.

I do believe that a person can struggle with homosexuality and still begin his or her pursuit of Christ. And no matter what, I will never stop being friends with gay people. I have visited friends after they went to prison for doing way worse things, so why would I end a relationship with a gay person just because he or she lives in a way I believe is contradictory to the way of Christ? Never once have I felt tempted to be gay from merely being around gay people. If I ever felt that way, I might change my stance.

I once went on a business trip with a co-worker and good friend who is homosexual, and we stayed in the same room. His name is Peter, and we are close friends to this day. When a partner in ministry heard that I was going to share a hotel room with Peter, he confronted me and told me I was going down a dark road.

"Really?" I asked.

I told him I have never had homosexual thoughts. Not only that, I'm so far on the other side, it is the reason I never want to go to prison. I saw Shawshank Redemption. As Morgan Freeman said, "Prison life ain't no fairy tale." I ignored the ignorant friend and went on the business trip. Peter and I had a great time and spent hours talking more about God and his love for all people than anything else.

Peter never once put the moves on me. And that means he has some self-discipline, too, because as I said earlier, I'm a looker! I kid—but really, why can't we have our beliefs and gay people have theirs without a political war? We need to stay on the bus and in the conversation with everyone. When we create a hostile world for people, how can we ever convince them of the real love God has for them? We aren't winking at sin, but lest you forget, we all still have our daily struggles. Maybe we can cut them some slack and attend their lives, go to their birthday parties, and love them with open arms. That's just my opinion, anyway.

Another big issue has to do with abortion. Normally, people with Judeo-Christian ethics agree that we are against it. I too believe it to be a very poor choice one can make. But what concerns me is the overall stance the church takes to take every fight to the legal system.

Not long after our church started, we had an older couple come and begin to put out anti-abortion literature on one of the guest services tables. A staff member saw what they were doing and immediately asked them nicely to remove it. They refused. It's in moments like these that I am called for. I asked them to remove it, and when they refused to do so, I confiscated the material. I'm a very big man, so they put up no fight.

They asked why I wouldn't try to get the word out to save human lives. I explained that I don't believe we can really legislate righteousness, so why put so much of the church's time and money to such a campaign? I tried to explain that even though I share the belief that abortion is wrong, I also know that God gives us all free will. The Bible clearly says that God sets before us life and death, blessing and cursing, and then he pleads with us to choose life. I would rather have a conversation with a woman contemplating abortion than spend the church's resources trying to get the Supreme Court to make a ruling that most people would only ignore.

The world is a small place now. If we pass a law against abortion, what's to stop any woman from getting on a plane, flying south, and crossing the border to get one there? We have to stay focused on getting hearts to know Christ. He alone helps us make decisions that laws could never stop. We have laws against stealing, laws against murder, and laws against driving drunk. Yet every single day, people ignore those laws. I've sat in rooms with theologians and pastors more educated and gifted than I'll ever be, we've debated this for hours, and I still believe to my core that the way to change a cultural norm is to reach one mind and heart at a time. In my humble opinion, the church would do more good at the back door of an abortion clinic with a blanket than at the front with a sign condemning these ladies.

I ended my conversation with that couple by saying that this church has a different belief system about how to deal with the abortion issue. As I turned to walk away, she said that the blood of the innocent was on my head and hands. She then asked for all her literature back. "Sorry, you had the chance to pick it up; now it's mine."

Later on that night, I sat around a fire pit on my deck with several of our senior staff members to brainstorm about creative ways to get close to women thinking of having abortions. We came up with a plan to reason with those in this tough position. Over the last two years, we have seen some real good come of it. I would love to go into detail, but we all felt we should keep it under the radar. It was a God idea we had around the fire that night that ironically was being fed by some very angry literature I picked up that morning.

Over time, I have made it more and more a point to stay out of politics. We have a church with as many Democrats as Republicans. When did Christianity become a political party? I work for a king. He's it. Every four years, we elect a new president, but God's reign never ends.

As a younger guy, I was up for any political fight. Now I see that my role is to be Christ's ambassador to all. He has love for all, and he has a way in which he wants us to live, because he really does know what's best for us. Many times it doesn't make sense to me right out of the gate, but he always proves his Word.

I hope I was somewhat clear in giving you my stance here. I can handle differing opinions and have even changed my mind on several issues due to vigorous debates with others, but what I can't stand is when I don't communicate well. It's an issue I have worked on for years. If you're going to be a leader in the body of Christ, you have to know how to relay a message clearly. And if you struggle with it, you may need to go to the free class that every local courtroom gives Monday through Friday.

Those Who Can't Do, Preach

"Do or do not. There is no try." -
Yoda

THERE ARE A FEW across-the-board truths I live by when it comes to starting and growing a church. One is that you better have a real prayer life. Two is that you better do things to get people in the door. And three, you better have a good speaker, or the show comes to an abrupt end.

I read an article recently that polled the biggest fears Americans have. The number one thing Americans fear is public speaking. Wow! I can think of, like, ten things that would be worse right off the top of my head: spiders, snakes, IRS audits, having to rock a comb-over. Look, the list could go on, but nonetheless, it shows the gap between most speakers' psyches and the general public's opinion about our profession.

You would think that since the vast majority of people would dread this job, we would get all kinds of grace and mercy. Nope! People will come up to me almost every Sunday after service and tell me a Scripture I should have used or that I should have made this point or that point in my sermon. I take it in stride now and let it go. I wasn't always this calm about it. When I first felt called into teaching, I was eighteen and had no experience. In fact, the whole God thing was so new to me that I felt uncomfortable even blessing the food. But I had this gut feeling that I was supposed to do it.

I asked to preach at the church I attended, and they asked how long I had been a Christian. "That's a good question. What time is it now?" Yeah, they wouldn't let me do it. So they did what most churches do, "You should go help in the youth. Be a youth leader, and we'll talk again when you are forty." So I went to do my time with the kiddos.

Now, if you're just starting out as a youth pastor, there are some things you will need. First, you need a Bible that looks worn but cool, covered with duct tape, blue jean fabric, or metal. Then you need a tattoo and maybe an earring or two. If you are a girl, you need a nose or lip piercing. And for every male, you must have some trendy facial hair. All of this works to say, "I'm cool, I'm older, and I'm spiritually relevant." I walked in with a King James Bible in one of those zippered covers with a fish on it. I was clean-shaven, and I had yet to get my first tattoo. I did, however, have both ears pierced, so that bought me a few weeks to get a new Bible and grow a soul patch.

I liked the kids but found them to be a tough audience. Starting with teens was a great experience for me because they are the rudest people on earth.

If you bore them, they will literally turn around and start conversations with their friends. After my second fifteen-minute talk, a youth came up to me and said, "Boy, you suck at this Bible teaching stuff."

It stunned me. I, in turn, told him he was an ass. He responded by saying I couldn't talk to him that way because I was a Bible teacher. "Not according to you," I said. At that point, an adult leader separated us. He asked me how long I had been a Christian. I again asked, "What time is it now?"

Slowly over the next two years, I honed my skills at keeping those little farts focused on God. And over time, the main leader began to take a little notice of me. I will never forget the moment he walked into the church gym after youth and told me that I was going to talk at the Wednesday night service in two days. I can only think that I felt like every minor league pitcher who was being sent up to the pros. "I'm going to the show!" was what I wrote in my journal that night. There were only a couple hundred people at Wednesday services, but it was my moment. I crafted my message and stole illustrations from Chuck Swindoll, T. D. Jakes, and Bill Hybels. I was ready to rock. The music blurred by, and I took my notes up to announce my presence with authority. I taught, used Scriptures, and even got a few laughs. I felt like I had rocked their world.

After the service was over, I felt spent. All my friends came up and said I did great. I was on cloud nine. And then I was approached by the wife of an elder. "Well, it wasn't earth-moving, but it also wasn't all that bad, either. If you preach about five hundred more times, you might become decent at it." Wow! Thanks, Mom. No, I kid. She wasn't my mom—or friend, or fan—but she was right. Teaching is one of those things that you need to do over and over until you learn to do it well. I licked my wounds and began to look for places to preach.

A friend who worked at an old folks' home opened the first door for me. He told me that they were always looking for activities to do with their residents. So almost every Sunday afternoon, I would travel between three different homes and do a Bible lesson. If you think kids are rough, man, this was brutal! Most were wheeled in and left there against their wills.

Some would throw fits and try to wheel themselves out. The staff just began to lock the brakes on the wheelchairs so as to thwart an escape. It truly was a captive audience. There were usually ten to fifteen people there, and three of them were really into it. I crafted the messages to incorporate some humor I thought they could relate to—i.e., dinosaurs—but in the end, it proved to be an exercise in humility.

Then one day, while preaching to Moses's classmates, a woman who had come to visit her mom liked what she had heard. She asked if I would come to a RV park in the next town over to speak to a group of Winter Texans. A Winter Texan is an older retired person from the north who has traveled south in an RV to wait out the colder months. I was stoked. I was moving from the super-old to just normal old.

So the following week, as I made my way to the park, I had it in my head that I would be speaking to a small handful of people—not so. Holy cow! There were a ton of them, and they all came in golf carts. They packed the rec room and sang hymns that I had never heard. They were a lively bunch compared to ones with respirators, so I had a good time.

However, when I finished, I was inundated with criticism on what they felt I got wrong. They even argued in front of me with each other. I realized that all these people came from every denomination in America. I had no real understanding what others believed. I spoke there all winter and was invited to many dinners.

I fell in love with those old fogies and was churched in what each denomination believed. It was an education I really needed, and it helped me make better jokes in my sermons by saying, "This next story is for the Methodists." Then all the Methodists would hoot and holler. When it would start raining, I would say, "Wow! It looks like God's for the Baptists today!" Corny? Sure, but I must admit that because of their love and feistiness, I fell in love with most denominations.

Around this time, I got another shot at the big show. This time, it was on a Sunday morning. This was it—my moment. I worked hard on my sermon and gave it my all. And wouldn't you know it—I had gotten better. There were even a few times that the very large crowd was laughing like crazy. Afterwards, people were generous with the compliments—everyone except that elder's wife. I saw her coming, no doubt to honor my skills.

I waited to be falsely humble in receiving her praise, so you can understand my shock when she said, "Well, you've gotten funnier and speak a little better, but you didn't really say anything to change a life."

What?! You're so mean! I thought to myself.

The next day, while sitting with a woman who was a spiritual mother to me, I recounted those harsh words.

"Can you believe what she said?" I asked, hoping for her to come to my defense.

Instead, she said that she agreed with the assessment.

"What? Are you all conspiring against me? That was the best I could do."

My friend said, "Sweetie, do you want the truth so you can grow, or do you just want to be praised?"

I thought longer than I should have and finally yielded to the idea of learning to teach well.

She told me she had jury duty the previous week and that while she was there serving, God told her to tell me to go watch how the lawyers argue cases. She said that the good ones use humor but also leverage it to make hard and real points.

I took her advice and spent many Thursdays in the county courthouse. I saw how the lawyers there held life, death, and freedom in their words. I realized that there was no real good that God could use from my humor if I didn't bring his truth in at the same time. I still make a lot of jokes in my messages, but I can tell you that I work hard to make them count for a real issue.

As I mentioned earlier in this book, one other thing that has helped me speak better is my preparation time. Once, I got the chance to talk to a very high-level pastor, and I asked him how long he worked on any one sermon. Ten hours. I decided to also do that each week.

When I told my spiritual mom, she said, "Sweetie, you should double it."

To this day, I prepare twenty hours for all my talks—trust me, I need to. I know I'm not the best speaker in the world, but I try really hard to not be the worst either.

Teaching every weekend gets old pretty fast, and to stay fresh is a struggle for everyone in this business. Over time, we are changing people's ideas about God and life. If we work very hard at it, we can even change an entire community. It was hard to see that my gifts and calling didn't reach full potential right away. I had to take a lot of criticism on the chin and keep coming. Most came from people who, deep down, wanted me to succeed. I met other critics who said they were just trying to help, but in reality, they had come to kill my dreams. Many looked like friends when they showed up … right up to the point that they removed their sheep's clothing.

Hater-Aid, the Vision Quencher

"Nothing is so good that somebody somewhere will not hate it."

-Pohl's Law

A COUPLE YEARS AGO, a man hired our odd jobs team to help him go through and pack his belongings for an international move. One bright Thursday morning, we began working in his basement, bringing up boxes and sorting out what things would be sold in a yard sale and what would make the trip. About thirty-five minutes into the job, Brian came out of the garage and was jumped by two police officers while four others had guns drawn on him. They handcuffed him and asked him how many others were in the house. Brian was floored—literally.

They moved their assault into the house, where they screamed and shouted for us to "Drop everything and get on the floor!" Everyone complied and was frisked—well, everyone except the man who had hired us. He was furious. He yelled at the police, and it soon became clear that this was obviously a mistake. After they made a halfhearted apology and released Brian from his bracelets, they left.

The homeowner, however, was not done. He stormed outside and began to holler at his older neighbor. As we went back to work, he began to share the whole story. He had bought the house ten years earlier, and it became clear that the guy next door was a hateful old man. After a few years and many verbal altercations, he had had enough and put the house up for sale, but it just never sold. His job required him to travel a lot, so he found freedom on his road trips. When the opportunity came up to move overseas, the big selling point for him was that he could get away from the neighbor who hated for no reason. We all sympathized with him, because who hasn't worked or lived near someone who, for whatever reason, hates you?

It is no different in church work. The sad reality is that usually over half of those who hate us are other Christians and Christian leaders. Not a month goes by that I don't read about how one famous pastor thinks the other one is fake or wrong about something. They shoot at each other in tweets, blogs, and sermons. It's sick. I guess I was just too naive when I became a Christian. I assumed we all cut each other slack and loved each other. Man, was I wrong.

The first experience I had with this was in my early years. I was looking for an article on Bill Hybels. I had read his book, Rediscovering Church, and instantly connected with his approach to reaching the lost. Who could shoot at that? In my search for the article, I came across many people criticizing him and calling him names. They said he was an awful leader, and some even went so far as to say that the people who attended his church were not really Christians. And these were from other men in ministry. What? I was shocked.

At that moment, I was suddenly aware that many of us are insecure and need to bring others low. It didn't take me long until I had my own list of enemies. They gossip and talk and judge. I really think many don't realize that their enemy makes sure their words find our eyes. I must admit I wasn't one of those tough guys who said it never bothers them.

At first, it caused me great pain. I even tried to reach out to some so we could heal our relationship, but to no avail. It was in one of these times of attack that I was in my time with God, bemoaning my lot in life. I felt God whisper to me that I needed to learn to ignore it and understand that if I was going to make a difference, then I was going to have controversy. He told me to embrace it, not just survive it.

Once, I was walking through the local Wal-Mart sports department and saw a mouthpiece that football players wear. I'm not sure why, but I felt I needed to buy one. I took it home, boiled it in water, and molded it to my mouth. It had been years since I played football, so the whole thing was bringing back some really fond memories.

And that's when God spoke to my heart. He said that I should keep that mouthpiece as a reminder of the life that he chose for me. "Any sport that requires you to wear a mouthpiece is one of violence." I wrote down Matthew 11:12: *"The kingdom of heaven suffers violence, and violent men take it by force."*

I like fighting, so I began to embrace this Scripture. In ministry, we go through seasons: seasons of building, seasons of growth, seasons of maturity, and of course, seasons of war. And when war time comes, I pull out that mouthpiece and wear it during my prayer time. I even put it in my pocket and take it to dicey meetings just to remind myself that I chose to do this, so I need to be all in.

One of the best pieces of advice I ever got about fighting was in my freshman year of high school. I wasn't a big kid, and for some reason, I was getting picked on. I was in more than my fair share of fights. After receiving one pretty bad butt-kicking, a senior pulled me aside.

He asked, "You get beat up a lot, don't you?"

"Yeah," I said. "I do."

He said, "What if I told you the secret to never getting beat up again?" I was all ears. He went on to say, "When two guys are about to fight, you can tell that one doesn't really want to be there. He has to be there, but his heart just isn't in it." I agreed that this is true, and then he dropped the bomb. "Never be that guy. Always want to be in the fight more." As stupid as that sounds, I rarely lost a fight again. I worked myself up to want to be there.

In our line of work, we are the invading army. We have come to take our communities back for Christ. When we started this church, rumors spread that we were a cult, too young, and not even Christians. We just kept right on moving forward. As you live your calling to the fullest, others will fight and oppose you. They will send you mean letters, gossip, and blog about you, your friends, and the church.

Life sucks sometimes; wear a helmet. Want the fight, want the criticism, and embrace the attack. Most times, it's simply the proof you are right in line with God's plan. And then choose to never get caught up in the drama. Make your plans, and move forward.

Success at any level collects haters. Don't let them distract you from the real enemy and his work. Sure, you will take some hits. Sometimes you will get nailed for your failures as well, but when you do, remember that those failures open the doors to some of the finest truths. Sometimes we need to fall in a hole.

A Man Falls in a Hole …

"You may have to fight a battle more than once to win it."
-Margaret Thatcher

Have you ever heard that old story about a man who falls in a hole—a deep one? He looks up and sees a priest walk by.

The man yells to the priest, "Help me, please. I have fallen in this hole."

The priest looks to heaven and says, "Dear God, please help this wretched man out of this hole."

He finishes his prayer and walks away.

A little while later, the man sees the local doctor walking by and begins to yell again asking for help. After carefully examining the problem, the doctor pulls out a prescription pad, scribbles something, tosses it down, and walks away. The man picks it up and reads the words, Get out of the hole.

Finally, about an hour later, the man sees his friend, Joe, walking by.

"Joe!" he yells. "Can you help me, please? I have fallen in this deep hole, and I can't get out!"

No sooner had those words left his mouth than Joe jumped down into the hole with his friend.

"Why did you do that, Joe? Now we are both stuck in the hole."

Joe replied with a smile, "That's okay. I've been in this hole before, and I know the way out. Follow me."

I love the simplicity of the tale. The truth is that we are always better at helping people through their failures when we have had to deal with failures ourselves. In building a church, everyone has setbacks and failures. Many times it can be easy to question if God is just not for us. When we can't raise the money for a project, when people leave the church, or when we fail at just getting them in the doors, it can feel like we must be outside of God's plan. The truth, however, couldn't be further from those thoughts. We need the storm to show us the cracks in our leadership or church. Even when you fail in front of your congregation, it can be a holy thing.

Just recently, our church bought forty-six acres next to the local high school. I'll explain more later about what it is being developed for. When we first talked to the owner, the price was close to $1.4 million. It is a beautiful piece of land with giant pine trees, a house and a barn, natural springs, and a huge meadow. We went to our tiny church and tried to raise the money, but we didn't even come close. A year later, the price had fallen to $975,000.

Again, we put on the full court press, and again, we came up completely short. One concerned member wrote me a letter suggesting that maybe

God was saying no to us because the money just wasn't coming in. It's something that our entire team had to debate. In the end, through much prayer and discussion, we felt that we would just keep coming at it every few months.

And then, in March of 2011, we called the owner. This time, the price of the land was crazy-low. We loaded up our cannons again as I explained to our church that we were going to keep coming at this until it either sold to another party or we got it. In a matter of less than two weeks, we had raised the $100,000 we needed to secure the land. People gave up to their eyeballs like never before. It was a God moment to see this part of our story happen.

In the next few weeks, calls began to come in from people in our church who said that watching us fail and yet keep on trying made them dust off some of their old dreams as well. If we would have gotten the land when we wanted it, we would have had to pay hundreds of thousands more than we did. God put that land in our heart, and we just ran at the door over and over until we busted through.

Now, I would be lying to you if I told you that each time we failed, I wasn't bummed out. The hardest part of being knocked down is making yourself get up again. But there are real rewards for those who do not lose their confidence. Just remember what Hebrews 10:35 says: "*So do not throw away your confidence; it will be richly rewarded.*" Don't let setbacks stop you.

Over time, we have come to see that because of how we do church, we are predisposed to failing more than others. In basketball, when you take a lot of shots, you may make a lot of baskets—but you also miss more. Don't let it intimidate you.

Every morning, I start with a shower. During this time, I like to pump up the music and rock out while lathering up. I sing and dance and quite often slip and fall. My wife thinks that this is the way I will come to my end. Yesterday, we calculated that in the last four months, I have slipped and fallen in the shower six times. She encouraged me to ditch the music and just get business done. A few falls here and there are fine with me, because most days, I get out ready to take on the day, talk to God, and love my family and friends. So I choose to embrace a life that may have some falls but evokes passion.

Isn't that the kind of church we want to build? We want churches that are pushing forward and making a difference. Even those of us in smaller communities want that. I never want to be just a paycheck player in the body of Christ. I want to leverage my time and position to reach people's hearts. I know that I will fall short many times, but I also know that every so often, something we do works in a really big way. In many ways, it's a numbers game with ideas and leading. The more you fall, the more you succeed. It's just that simple.

During our short existence in Conifer, we have learned that every day brings new challenges, joys, and fears. Daily, we are all learning the difference between our tactics and our mission. That realization has helped us run a better race. After all, when Paul talks about our race, what does he say? "Pace yourself"? Nope. He says, *"If you're going to run … win it."*

Every Morning in Africa ...

"Everything flows; nothing stays still."
-Heraclitus

SOMEONE GAVE ME A poster a few years ago. I'm sure many of you have seen one like it. It is a picture of a lion, and in the distance is a gazelle. Under the picture, the caption reads, "Every morning in Africa, a gazelle wakes up. It knows that it must run faster than the fastest lion, or it will be killed. Every morning, a lion wakes up. And it knows it must outrun the slowest gazelle, or it will starve to death. Now, it doesn't matter if you are a lion or a gazelle ... when the sun comes up, baby, you'd better be running."

I love those words. They boil many leadership principles down to a complete truth. I live by these words. Get moving!

I was recently looking online for the top ten biggest heists of all time. I was going to use them as a sermon illustration. I must admit, I am fascinated by a well-executed robbery. I love movies like Ocean's Eleven, The Italian Job, and The Heist. In my research, I found some pretty interesting heists.

One happened at the Boston Museum in 1990. Two police arrived at the museum and said they were responding to a disturbance on the property. Without question, they were let in, where they immediately handcuffed several security officers and went to work. In under an hour, they had taken a dozen paintings, including works by Degas and Rembrandt worth an estimated $300 million.

The biggest jewel heist happened in Cannes, France in 1994. Three men armed with machine guns entered the store as it was closing. Shouting and firing their guns, they took over $30 million in jewels and fled. Later it was discovered that their guns were loaded with blanks!

If you ever want a good read, look up these and more online. There are a ton of stories out there. As I was reading about various heists, I couldn't help but be taken aback by the intelligence and resourcefulness of those involved. Many times, plans had to change, and personnel had to be added. A few times, when tunnels were used to get to the goods, the thieves would have to change course. But even with setbacks, they pressed on toward the money.

I remember thinking about this one day and came up with what we now call Tactics vs. Mission Strategy. You see, in our church, we want to reach people. This is our mission. In order to do this, we employ many different plans and programs. These are our tactics. In any war, the goal stays the same— to win the war. But the plans and actions to secure the victory change based on where the enemy is and what he is doing. We try to stay flexible in our tactics but rigid in our mission.

Let me give you an example: one of the biggest outcries from our church when we started was to reach the teens in our community. They have their issues. To get near them is a hard sell, but nonetheless, we began to organize events and activities to get them in the door. We had some success, and now our youth group has over a hundred kids in it.

Along the way, we realized that many teens would just not come to a church youth group. So our staff started a Friday night gathering with games, sumo wrestling suits, jousting, and other activities that require a parental release form. We never mention God or even bless the food. It's just fun. Now, our mission is the same—to get those kids to know Christ. We had to take a step back and approach it a different way, though.

Many times during my early years in ministry when a plan or idea would fail, I would chalk it up to the fact that God was just not in it. Over time, I have come to the stark realization that God wants us to reach people. He hasn't changed his mind about that, so we all must use the minds Christ has given us to think of new ways to do it. If we fail at something numerous times, we just have to rethink our approach, not our mission.

I had a friend who told me a story about an eighteen-wheeler that was driving down a highway at about sixty miles an hour. The truck had to go through a tunnel that, unfortunately, was two inches too short for his load. The truck plowed into it and was completely stuck. They brought engineers in from all over the state, but for two days, they were at a loss for how to get it unstuck.

Finally, a twelve-year-old boy in a passing car yelled, "Why don't you let the air out of the tires?"

They did, and wouldn't you know it—it gave them just enough relief to pull it out.

Many times, we need to take a step back, come up with another plan, retool, and then retry. Winning in any arena in life is about being able to overcome challenges. Every ministry event we have ever done has brought new issues and problems out that we never saw coming. We are at war, so we shouldn't be surprised that the enemy has counter moves. The idea is to always be growing wiser, learning more, and charging up the hill again. People's forevers are at stake.

We spend a lot of time looking at what other churches are doing around the country. Many of them are ahead of us, so we don't try to replicate the wheel. We call them, ask questions, and try to learn from their tactics as well. I know many pastors who feel that if they didn't think of it, then it's not a good idea. If you have that mindset, then you really are limiting what your church can do. I believe that if you take ideas from the best and make them your own, everyone wins.

So decide if you're the gazelle or the lion, and then run accordingly. Ministry is not a job that tolerates weakness very long. You have to understand that God has made us able to fulfill the call he has for each one of us. At times, he requires that we stand alone. Sometimes we are the ones everyone is looking to. A few times in all our lives, we have to live heroically.

You Better Find Your Phone Booth

"Aspire rather to be a hero than merely appear one."

-Baltasar Gracian

IF YOU HAVE NEVER had someone break into your house in the middle of the night, then you're just missing out on one of the most exciting things in life. Several years ago, my wife and I had such an experience. We lived in a two-story house, and all our bedrooms where upstairs. At about 2:00 in the morning, I got a call on my cell phone. It was from a friend who was crashing on our couch downstairs.

With a muffled voice, he said, "Michael, someone's breaking into the house."

I told him to stop them, to which he replied in a whisper, "No way!"

At this point, I jumped up and informed Amy as to what was going on downstairs. I told her to call 911, and I would go confront our visitors. With my wife and kids in harm's way, I felt a wave of anger come over me.

As I took off for the door, Amy said, "Hey, put a shirt on!"

When I sleep, I only wear shorts and socks only, so she tossed me a sweatshirt—her sweatshirt. Now, let me take this time to explain to you the size difference between Amy and me. I was, at that time, a six-foot, one-inch, 280-pound man who lifted weights religiously. She was about a quarter of my size.

In the dark and with adrenaline pumping, I pulled the sweatshirt on that covered just my chest and half of each arm. I came down the stairs and turned to go through the kitchen. Unfortunately, the wooden floors gave me no traction in my socks. I began to run in place. As I finally reached the front door, one man was already in. Within a moment, I had him pinned to the floor just as the police pulled up. His friends were captured too.

Just sheer desire to protect my family had overridden every ounce of fear. When I came back to bed, Amy took one look at me in that shirt and busted out laughing. However, for the next few days, every time she saw me, she would say, "There's my hero!" I must admit it felt good. I had faced fear and lived to tell the tale. The truth is that none of us would have respect for a man who would not get up to protect his family. That was my job. We had never discussed it before we were married, but it was understood.

There is a lot you aren't ready for when you get married. No one told me that when I picked a side of the bed, it would be forever! I just said, "This side will do." I didn't measure where the TV was or how close to the bathroom it put me. I just picked. But in protecting my family, I just knew that I was the one who would fight—and if necessary, die—for those I love.

The truth is that if you want to be good in any level of ministry, you're going to have to succeed in moments that freak others out. And just like Superman, you will have to dive into a phone booth and come out a stronger version of yourself. You will have defining moments where you cannot flinch or pull back.

Everyone around you will be watching you in those moments, and they will mimic you. If we are cowards or hide from our responsibilities, they will lose respect for us. But if you stand your ground, many will join you, being inspired by your courage. It is a true statement that courage can become such a part of our lives that it becomes a habit. Let me illustrate.

Our church was started in the local high school. After about a year and a half there, the school district, hurting for money, kept raising our rent to unbelievable highs. In the last few months we were there, they even charged us for the use of the hallways that lead to the auditorium. It became insane, but they had us.

You see, in our town, there is literally nowhere else to meet. If we couldn't afford the school, we were sunk. At this time, we had also rented a 12,000-square-foot building that accommodated our diner and church offices. Upstairs was completely gutted and could only seat two hundred people at best. In order to save money, we decided to move to two services and hold them there.

While we completed our contract with the school, we made the upstairs of our building usable. But four days before our first service, we were told that the church couldn't meet there because it was zoned wrong. It was too late to go back to the high school, so we felt paralyzed. My young and very driven staff members felt like they had been kicked in the gut. The county had said no way, and that was it.

I must admit that I too felt a wave of panic crash over me—but I also knew that I couldn't show that to my staff. I excused myself to my office. We would come together again in two hours, and I would have a plan. I confidently walked back to my office and closed the door. I said one simple prayer: "A little help, God. Please." I sat down and called the county. I had to go through nine people before I finally talked to a very kind, sane man who was willing to work with us. We got a temporary permit and had to jump though some hoops, but we were in.

I strolled into the meeting with my staff like I hadn't a care in the world. I told them who I had talked to and sent a couple of the girls to the county office to get our permit. I took that time to encourage them all to stay up and focused when setbacks come. "God is in this. God is in this." And with that said, I went back to my office and threw up. Wow! That was close. I may not be a hero, but I play one in my church. Sometimes you have to reach deep inside your soul and find that courage when others are losing theirs.

Many times, we feel the discouragement and pain more than those around us. It still doesn't change the rules. The truth is that if you ever want to be great, then from time to time, you're going to have to do whatever it is you do while hurt. You'll have to win a battle with a limp or wound. You have to be the front person.

And the truth is this: it doesn't always have to be the highest leader in an organization. Many times, our church has moved forward by the leadership and passion of a staff member who refused to say die. These people get in our faces and remind us what's at stake and who we are. They make us rise up into the leaders and people we always thought we could be.

One thing that has helped me with this was something that a high school coach told me my sophomore year. I loved football but was less than excited about being on the kickoff team. Hitting each other at close range was fine, but to run twenty yards full speed into each other seemed insane. My coach noticed that I took a lot of hits worse than I needed to. He tried to explain that if I went full speed, then the defense would get the brunt of the collision.

I confessed that I was honestly too scared to do that. And then he gave me some words of wisdom that have helped me through life.

"Michael," he said, "you'd be stupid not to be afraid. Collision is not a normal act, but just do it scared anyway, and do it at full speed."

And I did.

Leadership can have its moments that reveal who we are. We have to seize those moments. When I was a firefighter, we were constantly practicing scenarios at the training tower so at a moment's notice, we would be able to act accordingly. One of our captains had a favorite saying. "Hesitation is the mother of all screw-ups." He knew that every time we were called, minutes count. To not act would cause bad things to get worse. At one such training session, a very new recruit mouthed off to him.

"Relax! It's just practice."

Our captain asked him what his last job was; he had been a cook at a food chain. The captain told him that if he had a bad day at Burger World, someone might get their order wrong.

"But if you have a bad day here, son, someone dies—and that is just unacceptable."

When church leadership breaks down and cannot overcome, the fallout is immeasurable. Many times, we may not know the extent of it this side of heaven. People's forevers are at stake, and we have to understand that we are accountable for our behavior and actions through the toughest times.

We are called by God to be overcomers, to win the race, and to lead with all diligence—to win by attrition. We must wear our big boy pants and bring our lunch all day, every day. We have to become strong in the weak places, and when it looks like everything is falling down, we must stand. I know many ministers who have done so, and in the end, God rewarded them for their grit and determination. May their tribes increase!

Leading in adversity usually falls in the hands of key people on the team. But the truth is that a church that wants to grow rapidly has to get its people to buy in and get involved. For every one staff member we have working in this church, there are dozens of volunteers making it all run like a well-oiled engine. They are the real engine that powers the work. They are our heroes.

Blood, Sweat, and Volunteers

"If you want to build a ship, don't drum up people together to collect wood and don't assign them tasks and work, but rather teach them to long for the endless immensity of the sea."
-Antonio de Saint-Exupery

ACH WEEK, THEY SHOW up to church an hour early: businessmen, schoolteachers, firefighters, police, contractors, mechanics, and teenagers. Some meet to go over the day's Sunday school lesson. Others get two-way radios and position themselves around the property to help park cars and greet visitors. In the diner, food is being prepped by a Lockheed Martin engineer, a police captain, and two single moms who work two jobs to make ends meet. This is the church I get to lead, and the people here have taught me more about hard work than any life lesson I could share. And the truth is that without them, their driven work ethics, and their great attitudes, our church would not be nearly as successful. They are my heroes.

We learned really fast that to reach a community, we needed to be a community. We need more workers. Even Jesus saw this coming. He said that the harvest is plentiful, but the workers are few. Jesus saw the need for many people to take a real role in the body of Christ.

At The Journey, we encourage every person to serve in one area of ministry. Now, like any church, you're going to have people who come out strong and want to do it all, but over time, pull back from serving. I believe that all Christ-followers have a built-in desire to do things that help the body grow. I also know that we have a bent toward putting God further and further back on the burner. Many fall off the volunteer radar pretty quickly ... and so it goes. But what we have found here is some simple truths that have helped us get and keep a good amount of volunteers.

First, we often ask the whole church to plug in and help somewhere. Many times, people have to be asked several times before they finally jump in. It always amazes me when a person who has attended our church for a while approaches to ask where they could get involved. We have so many ministries that I can't even remember them all, yet they seemed to have missed this. Every three months, we make a push and ask our congregation to give a little of their time each week. And every time we do, we get more.

Second, we try to steer people toward their passion and away from what they hate. A lady once approached us and said that she was ready to serve in the children's ministry. She looked less than excited about it, so the staff member pointed out the lack of enthusiasm. She explained that she had previously worked in children's church and hated it, but she thought that God was going to make her do it to teach her patience. Yikes! Those poor kids!

Our staffer asked if she had any passions that she could use in the church.

"You know, like a job you don't dread."

The woman said she really liked old people.

"Super! We have several who need love and assistance during the week and in our services."

She jumped in with both feet. Can you imagine how long she would have lasted in a ministry she hated?

It's true that sometimes people have to serve in areas that are not exactly where they want to be. Sometimes you just need the help. It's in those times that you need mature Christians who can do a good job with a great attitude until help arrives. But over time, you have to try and steer people into areas where they love to serve. They need to have a passion for it, or they will just lose momentum.

We also teach from the pulpit on a regular basis the importance of involvement. For many Christians, the desire to help is overrun by the pace of their lives. God matters to them in theory, but they can't seem to reprioritize their lives to make it happen—and round and round we go. Sometimes we have to challenge people to do the hard thing.

When someone says, "I want to help here or there, but I just don't have the time," then "Sure you do" is my normal answer.

Look, if God is prompting you to get involved in a

ministry or an act of service, it is up to you to change your whole life around to do it. People who do this find a reward that ignites the rest of their lives. People who don't live lives of frustration, because in their hearts, they know that they were built for more than they have become.

One last thought on volunteers: love them. I mean it. Write them notes, mention them in sermons, and give them high-fives. Sure, the high five is from the 80s, but it's still got worth for them. You are the only paycheck they want for their time. They want you to tell them they are changing lives and helping the hurt.

The truth is that every job is important in the body of Christ, and it is the leadership's job to remind volunteers of this on a weekly basis. Feed them constant encouragement, and they will stick around for the long haul. Many of them might even someday become part of the paid staff—and then the fun really starts!

Waiting for Uncle Pete to Die

"Experience is the name everyone gives to their mistakes."

-Oscar Wilde

AH, THANKSGIVING. We all have memories from our childhood. Many are full of warm thoughts and smells. Mine, however, were a bit darker. When I was growing up, we used to do Thanksgiving at my step-grandparents' house. It's a whole other complicated story for another time. But anyway, we would all come together, and the tables were already set.

There was one giant table for the adults. They had real dishes, and all the food was kept there. It was in the dining room, where my grandfather could have a clear view of the TV in the next room. My grandfather never turned off the TV for any reason whatsoever. The kids were put at several folding tables in another room. I'm not sure what normally went on in this room, but it always smelled like moth balls and feet—not the best dining atmosphere. And to top it all off, the worst part was that we didn't have our own TV to watch.

As the years progressed and the elderly members of the family began to make their way to God, I became aware that the older kids got to take the place of the dead relatives. It was like some kind of morbid Thanksgiving draft. One year, I was the oldest kid left, and my sister said, "You're next, Mike." Awesome! I took a long look at the generation before me and picked my horse. Uncle Pete looked bad—really bad. The man smoked and drank, and on top of that, no one in the family liked him. My family also has some temper issues, so there was a good chance of things going to fisticuffs at the drop of a hat, making my odds even higher.

Over the next year, I waited for the news of his sad departure. Once he was even hospitalized. But he didn't die that year or the year after that. In fact, he may still be alive to this day! After my mom and stepdad divorced, I lost track—but needless to say, I never made it to the adult table. What can I say? Sometimes the journey of a thousand miles comes to a tragic end because people don't know when to stop breathing. I was young and a pagan. I'll admit they were dark goals. But that grown-up table was alluring.

Now, this is a word for all you younger leaders out there who want to go into church work: it may suck for a while. Sometimes it feels like you're at the kids' table too long. You want to move up and do bigger things. It tests your patience and your will—I know. I was in the same place. In your mind, you may even start to wonder when in the world you'll get your chance.

Here is my advice to you: One, do what you have been given to do very well. You'll hear this from everyone around you, but that's because it is true. You must be faithful with the little; there is no shortcut home on this one.

Two, learn more than you already know. Listen to podcasts of leaders who are at the peak of their game in ministry. Read books on leadership and growth—and not all have to come from the Christian bookstore. Many leaders in the military and business world have a lot to offer, so indulge.

And three, if it looks like you will never get used, get going. In heaven, God will never drag some leader to the front of the line to give an account for why he or she held you back from your calling. Some leaders are just too insecure to launch Joshuas out onto the stage. It's not worth trying to win them over. Just go do what it is God called you to do.

And now a word for us senior guys: look, I know how agitating young leaders can be. They know it all and can do it better than you. They think you are standing in their way to become all that God has called them to be. But remember that whether or not they know it, they need you. The list of men and women I wore out in my climb to do church is long and filled with hurts. But in the end, I am glad for every tough conversation—and even for being held back. Someday they will thank you. But along the way, maybe consider giving them bigger roles.

We have all been in a church where it is preached that God can use you no matter how young you are, but when you look around, you can't find a person under thirty doing anything except working with the youth or playing backup in the band. I believe that what defines leaders is not what they do with their lives but rather what they helped others around them do with their lives. Look at David's mighty men. When they got to him, they were literally the dregs of society, and they became generals, warriors, and mighty men—all because their leader put them in situations to grow.

What can it hurt, really? I once put a nineteen-year-old kid in a room with a couple that had been married for twenty-two years. Neither the teenager nor the couple knew I was going to do that.

I walked in with him and said, "This is Cortland, and he's going to counsel you."

They stared in disbelief and anger. The woman asked his age and then commented that they had been having problems longer than he was alive.

"So what?" I asked, and I walked out.

Guess what happened? He did fine. They even met with him several more times and are still married to this day. You may think that's foolish, but I had met with this couple several times, and they wouldn't listen to any counsel. If they were intent on ending their marriage, then at least I could give my very young staff some much-needed experience in the process.

And what if he would have given them bad counsel? Well, who knows? They had done a pretty damn good job of screwing up their own lives and those of their kids. At some point, you can't make things much worse. But I also know Cortland's heart. He loves people, loves God, and isn't the kind of person to pull punches, so I let him out of the cage.

Many on my staff do things that are above their

pay grade, and at times, they make mistakes or even give bad counsel. They say sorry and learn from it, but I have to let them do it, or they never learn. I think often of Samuel in the Old Testament. The Bible said each year his mom would bring him a linen ephod to wear while he was growing. I'll bet every year when she put the new one on him, it was a bit too big, and by the time she returned again, it was a bit too small.

The same goes for our calling. We grow into and even past certain levels in our life. Also, if you make room for the Joshuas, they are less likely to split your church or knock you down. They will love you for it and fight and win battles you never could win. Don't make them wait at the kids' table. The kingdom of God could use the help.

Forty-Six Acres, Ten Chainsaws, and a Little Elfin Magic

"Buy land. They're not making it anymore."
-Mark Twain

I HAVE A CLOSE friend named Brian. He is a big man—very big. If a normal man was the size of a doughnut, he would be a Cinnabon. And to match his size is his coolness. My staff and I often say that when we grow up, we want to be Brian. The man knows everything and everyone and owns one of everything ever made.

"Hey, Brian, you know where we could rent a bulldozer?"

"Rent one? I got one."

"Hey, Brian, you know anyone who has a walk-in cooler where we could store an entire buffalo we just killed?"

"Yep, I do."

"Hey, Brian, you know where we could hide a body?"

"Yep. Just let me get my shoes!"

"Hey, Brian, we are going to climb this mountain. You want to go?"

Brian says, "No, you're not. It's about to rain."

"What?" I ask. "The sky is clear." Bam! Lightning hits one hundred yards away, and Brian laughs. He's awesome.

Not long ago, we were getting a tour of his new home. It looks like a home from MTV's Cribs, and the view is unbelievable! But what caught my eye was that he had put a urinal in every bathroom next to the toilet.

"You can do that?"

"Sure. Why not? Now I never again have to hear my wife say to put the seat down."

On many levels, Brian is a genius in his no-nonsense approach to life. He is the kind of guy who doesn't overthink things. He's just logical. He is a loving father, husband, and a heck of a business man, and you can tell it all comes from his very practical approach to life.

I can't tell you how much that practicality will help you when you build a church. People have needs. If you meet their needs, then you get to be near them. If you get near them, then you can become friends. And if you become friends, then you might be there to introduce them to God.

It was this practical approach that led us to the land we recently bought—46.6 acres in the Rocky Mountains. The land borders the high school and two major roads. Over two-thirds of it is covered in giant pine trees. For those of us from Texas, it looks like we live in the middle of a huge Christmas tree lot. It is absolutely beautiful.

One of our desires is to build a rec center up here. On Sundays, we would use the gym and other facilities for church. The rest of the week, the community would have access to it. It's a massive project and one that would just be a bit more than a church of five or six hundred could do. Several of our staff members have been taking online courses to learn how to write grants. There is a lot of grant money out there that even churches can get if we go after it. That is the long-term outlook.

The land, however, has immediate uses. In the first few weeks after we bought the land, a ton of volunteers from the church came and cleared a walking path around the property. It is a beautiful pathway that is almost a mile in length. We have cleared dead trees and are building an obstacle course, a zip-line, a fort, a climbing wall, and an amphitheater that seats three hundred.

We have just installed a disc golf course around the property and are making plans to make a clearing for a massive sledding hill. Hidden throughout the walking trail are numerous garden gnomes for families with young kids to find. The idea behind all of this is to turn our land into a community park— open to all, every day. We are planning for the grand opening to be in mid-August. We can't wait.

This is our biggest endeavor to date, and we are really excited about it. The work to get it ready is impressive, but we are pushing to get it all done. It's a God thing that we even got the land. We drove past this place every week for at least a year and asked God to help us get it. Never tell me that prayer doesn't work, because I have seen God do the impossible firsthand.

I just wanted to share this small bit of our story. I think there are many churches in smaller communities that could reach more people if they used their building and properties to get proximity. For us, it's a fun adventure, and honestly, our staff and church will get as much use out of this park as the community. If you're ever in our neck of the woods, come on up, and I'll play a round of disc golf with you. You better bring you're a-game with you, though; I'm pretty good at it now.

Knowing Your Soulish System

"You don't have a soul. You are a soul. You have a body."

-C. S. Lewis

HAVE YOU EVER GONE swimming with dolphins? I have, and believe me, it is not as cool as it sounds. I was just out of high school and spending a few days with some friends on South Padre Island in South Texas. We decided to walk out to the end of the jetties. These are long rock walls extending way out in the ocean that create a channel for boats, barges, and ships to come through the bay side.

It took quite a while, but we finally got to the end. Big, foamy waves crashed onto the rocks. Various sea creatures were everywhere, but what caught our eyes was a school of dolphins feeding about fifty yards off the rocks. The conversation quickly turned to how cool it would be to swim with them. After all, we all grew up watching Flipper. They're harmless

… right?

We took off all our clothes and jumped into the very cold, murky water en route to play with these cute sea creatures. Now, I'm a pretty fast swimmer, so I led the charge. I arrived at what I felt was the last place that they had surfaced. I treaded water for about two minutes, and then it happened. One of these giant animals surfaced about a foot in front of me. He brushed past me and knocked me back like I was a piece of driftwood.

It was at that moment I realized I was in the ocean with a very large mammal, and that these finned species have teeth! He was not Flipper; he was not fun. He was all business, and I felt like I needed to get out of his world. From land, they looked fun and small. Up close and personal, they look like five hundred pounds of serious business.

My swim back was the closest I've ever come to running on water. I looked like a duck taking off. I climbed out of the ocean cold, naked, and grateful to be living on land. It's true that my life was probably never in that much jeopardy, but the whole experience made me feel more educated and more alive. Was it stupid? Yes, but I'm still talking about it to this day! I had lived; I had not died. My food that afternoon tasted better than ever before. The world's colors popped! I had gotten my heart racing and done something different.

Now, I could fill pages with tales of adventures I had growing up and into my early twenties. Then, suddenly, the stories stop. When I got into ministry, I began to lose the passion to do new things and have fun. Let's be honest—church work at every level is about others. We can run ourselves, our family, and staff members into a bleak wall of monotony and passionless existence. For me, it happened slowly over the years.

Then one day, I realized I was emotionally numb. It was like having a type of leprosy of the soul. I didn't laugh, I didn't cry, and I didn't find fun in life. Life had become all about my duties as a husband and father and in my job; it was my cross to bear. So what takes fun loving, passionate people and turns them into the spent? That's a good question. Here's what knocked me down:

Letting other people decide what is and is not appropriate for me to do.

As a young pastor, I trained and engaged in cage fighting. Back then, it was a new sport that most thought was barbaric. Today, the UFC has begun to overshadow boxing, but then it was not as popular. I was very careful and secretive about it, because I knew some people in my life who mattered would not understand. Luckily, I was in the fire department at the same time, so it was easy to explain away scratches and bruises. For me, it was about my love of fighting. I didn't hate the other guys I was fighting. In fact, we all became very close friends. I found the whole thing to be very cathartic.

So, long story short, some of the people found out about my fighting. A few were very offended that their friend, a Christian leader, got in fights—on purpose—every Tuesday and Friday night. I visited with several of those who had issues with it and tried to explain, but in the end, it was no use. They were not fighters, so they really could not understand.

After much counsel with a man I respected, he encouraged me to quit, citing 1 Corinthians 9 about the issue of meat sacrificed to idols. So I quit. I took off my gloves. I conformed to the standard that the crowd needed me to be, because in the end, I wanted the growth of my church to continue.

What I was unaware of was that the growth had stopped in me. The church kept growing … as did my weight, anger, and frustration in my life. Things I loved to do had to go so I could look the part of a pastor. It wasn't until later that a Christian counselor explained to me that it was okay to have hobbies and do things that I enjoyed.

He said, "Michael, God made you a fighter. I encourage you to do what you enjoy. If you don't fight, then your soul will turn into a civil war."

Close friends know my hobbies, and they are cool with it. My life is now fun and meaningful again. When what I do rubs someone the wrong way and he or she leaves my church because of it, I have to let him or her go, because my life has to be sustainable.

No Down Time

I'm talking about weekly time to veg—to stare off in the corner, read a book for fun, or listen to some James Taylor or Van Halen (either are good choices). It should be a time to decompress. Chuck Swindoll quotes an Indian proverb that I love. It says, "You will break the bow if you keep it always bent." Working out, family time, dates with your spouse, and studying spiritual matters don't count in this area. You need to get away from everyone. Turn the phone off and refuse to check e-mail.

Jesus was constantly getting away, yet most of us

in ministry feel guilty doing it. *My inbox is too full* is our excuse. Let me tell you something we all know anyway: the inbox will never be empty. If you live a full life, you will die with your inbox still full. You have to stop the storm in your life once a week, or you will get seasick.

Just last week I was in the middle of a crisis—budget shortfalls and staff exits, not to mention all the other duties that we all have to deal with daily. To make matters worse, I have been building sermons on the book of Romans and was feeling less and less inspired. After staring at the wall in my office for over an hour, I packed up and went home. I worked out and took a shower. I saw my wife's US Weekly magazine on the chair in our room, turned my phone off, and began to read up on all the latest Hollywood gossip. I laughed. I cried. It moved me!

I read for over an hour and then flipped through the channels and watched the last part of The Green Mile and one episode of Top Chef. I came out of my room three or four hours later a new man. Sometimes your soul craves the normal—the void of drama. The next day, I felt God's Spirit inspiring me and directing me as I built sermons. The soul needs to be fed fun and freedom, or it begins to dry up.

Fear of Men

I covered this before, but let me say it once more. Those who work in ministry care for others, so at times, we can start to care too much what people think. This is what the Bible refers to as "the fear of man," and it is a snare and a trap that will only cost us in the end. I know I have a tendency to manage unhappy churchgoers very quickly. I spin it in my head as damage control. People can throw fits about a ton of things, and I have a tendency to want to fix the situation before it spreads to others. I fear that it could get bigger.

Over time, God has led me more and more to let people throw their tantrums—to let them say stupid or even mean things unchecked. God really can protect his church. He doesn't always need me as the goalie. It can be exhausting trying not to tick off anyone. Besides, you will never truly succeed at it.

We recently started a Saturday night service. We spent a lot of time talking to other churches and friends in ministry in order to find out what time would be good for the new service. The overall consensus was 5:30 p.m. That way, people still had time to go out with family and friends, and those with little children could get them fed and in bed at an early hour. It went over well … with almost everyone.

The following week, a woman stopped me in the hallway of our offices and told me 7:00 or 8:00 would've been a better time. I tried to explain that much time and discussion had gone into this decision and thanked her for her interest. The service would stay at 5:30 p.m. She then demanded to know who exactly we had talked to. I could have listed off the names of several other churches and clinched it with "Willow Creek does it!"

My staff and I love that particular church and the information that they have made available to us, so we throw their name around when we are trying to prove a point. But instead, I turned around and said, "We talked to The United Brotherhood of It's None of Your Business." Sure, it was rude; that was the point.

This lady is always taking on the entire staff about every decision. We have always tried to be nice and calm her down, but in the end, it hadn't helped. So we came up with a new plan—unfiltered honesty.

After my comment, she stood there in shock. I told her that everyone was tired of her criticism and negativity. I told her to get involved or bless some other church with her wonderful attitude. She was practicing the cheapest of all gifts—pointing out problems. She was better than this! But the truth was that we all dreaded her visits. I walked off, and she stormed out. The funny thing is that she never said a word to me about that day, but rather began being kinder and more encouraging to everyone. We really like having her around now, and she even looks brighter!

I have come to realize that I can never help anyone I'm afraid of. It's our responsibility to give people the truth in love. Yes, love—but it's also truth that people need to hear. It is freeing and also helpful. You may lose people if you do this, but the truth is that if you don't lose some people in ministry—well, you're not really trying hard enough.

Okay. So how do I build my soul? What do I do to keep a fresh and fun life?

Do what you love

I have come full circle back to what matters. I do the things that I love to do. Now, of course, this does not include sinning. But I have come to realize that cage fighting is fine if it is what you like to do. Everyone has bents and desires. Every one of you have things that you enjoy—hobbies and activities that you love and that, in turn, feed your soul. Be open about it with your congregation.

I have found that most people understand the need for me to be a whole person and not just a ministry machine. I refuse to hide my life anymore. These are the ABCs of me. If you don't like me, that's cool, but we aren't dating. I'm not going to fake it with the church. The church is a place that should love those who enjoy knitting, skydiving, fighting, and playing chess. We need to love the nerdy, popular, and unpopular alike. Here you have a home, but it's our home too. Be who you are, do what you love, and let the church body feel the weight of your passion!

Do unspiritual things on purpose

I had an epiphany one day. I ain't Moses. I live in a different world than him. I have never worn a robe, had a beard, or been to Egypt. I do, however, have a staff! But that is about where the similarities end. The funny thing about Christians is that we want our leaders to be the kind of Christians that we ourselves don't have the time or discipline to be. People need us to be Moses, David, or even Jesus, but we just can't be. And if you let yourself, you can feel the pressure to only do things with spiritual purpose—only read spiritual books, only listen to Christian music, or pray for hours on end. It may sound like I'm repeating a point from earlier in this chapter—and I am—but it should be beaten into all of our minds. Stop the merry-go-round and be human for a while—even often.

During the early days of starting the church, we had very little money. So every week, we played a game called *What do we need to keep the most?* That particular bill would get paid, and everything else was put off until we got our hands on more cash. Many times, the Internet was turned off.

This was tough for a staff of young adults in their twenties. Most of us had laptops, so when we had no Internet, we would go for a drive. We would sit in store parking lots crammed into a fifteen-passenger van using the free Wi-Fi! Everyone got his or her church stuff done quickly, and then we would watch YouTube sketches that made us laugh, check movie times, and download music. More than once, we were asked to leave.

Now, it's been a while since things got that tight, so we are legal surfers now. But those of us who had to go looking for Wi-Fi connections talk about it with fondness. We were just a bunch of kids having fun and living life. We need to keep those fun days around. Do some crazy, unspiritual, soul-ish things. Stay up too late from time to time. Play a prank on a staff member. I do this as often as I can. Buy some gadget you've put off buying. Go to a movie that in no way will help you grow as a person. Even if it is something that may make you look like a kid, do it anyway.

A note for preachers and teachers

This chapter is very important for all of us who speak often. Your passion for life will come out in your talks. If you are dry, they will be dry. However, if you are really living, then in turn, your sermons become alive. You can't fake happiness and passion long.

And now a few last random diddles before we say good night.

The Junk Drawer

"There are certain things men must do to remain men."
-Captain James T. Kirk, Commander of the starship Enterprise

IN MY HOUSE, WE have a drawer in the kitchen called the junk drawer. It has everything we need to live: matches, tape, batteries, a whoopee cushion, ramen, and Taco Bell sauce packets from 1988—everything. When we don't know what to do with something but feel we need to keep it, we put it in there.

Welcome to the junk drawer of this book. It's the end, and we thought there were a few lessons or things that we want to say before our time is over. They don't fit anywhere else, so we bundled them up with no rhyme or reason, and we leave them with you. Enjoy these tasty delights. They are in no particular order.

Okay, first of all, never send e-mails out without

blind copying everyone. Let me tell you about a bad day. We had a lady who once attended our church, and it quickly became clear she had some issues going on upstairs. I'm sure the confessed drug use didn't help matters. We loved on her and tried to help her through her struggles. We even helped her financially a few times, but we didn't see any effort on her part; we felt we were creating dependence instead of helping her change. One day, she asked for more money, and our team said no. They explained to her that the reason we couldn't give her money was that she was not getting help or trying to get out of this life she had.

Now about this time, our church had about a hundred people. We tried to get everyone to sign guest cards so we could keep them updated with the weekly events of The Journey. Unfortunately, the media team always sent out the e-mail with everyone's e-mail addresses showing. This lady began to e-mail the entire church spam, unwanted forwards, and other weird stuff. She demanded that the church send her on a trip to Rome along with other outlandish requests. People in our church could clearly read in the e-mail that this lady needed help, but it was still a valuable lesson. Take care not to make your mailing list public. Someday, someone will leave your church mad. They will want to grind an axe; don't give them this platform. We were very blessed that this person showed the weakness in our system, but I have friends in ministry with horror stories that don't end with a happy conclusion.

Second of all, you need to find people who balance you. For our team of young dreamers, it was the addition of Jim and Daphne. This couple came to us months after we started. They are in their late forties and have lived in the mission field for over twenty years.

Daphne epitomizes the godly woman. She also has a wonderful English accent, so everything sounds better coming from her. What is it with that accent? She could call you an idiot, and it would feel like a compliment.

Jim made the move from a director for Campus Crusade in France to a Colorado mountain man in record time. Weeks after joining our team, he called me one afternoon to ask if I wanted a ton of elk meat. I asked him who his dealer was, as hunting season was over. He proudly explained that he was called by a friend who was on the scene of an elk massacre. A Jeep had taken out five elk while driving, and the locals had already caught wind of it. That's right, folks—a lot of the people up here eat road kill. Jim instantly joined their ranks. I have not yet been able to overcome my common sense to venture into this dark practice, but Jim is wearing me down about the practical nature of it all.

Anyway, back to the point—this couple came at the perfect time to help balance our team. They bring a maturity and understanding that you can only get with years of serving God. Now, understand this— they are not passive. They love to push forward and are huge risk-takers. They also have a wealth of experience that brings real wisdom into our plans. If you can find people who have your same heart but a different temperament to help round out your team, they are critical to a growing church or ministry.

Next, read everything. I even dare you to venture out of the religious section. There are books on military and business leadership that can sharpen your claws for the future ahead. One of my closest friends in the world is a crazy guy named Steve. He is a self-made man. This guy reads a lot. I mean it—it's strange. I thought I was an avid reader until I met him.

His work requires him to travel a lot, and every time he comes back, he'll say, "Hey, I just read this or that, have you read it yet?"

No, Steve, some of us can't read a book in thirteen minutes, but I'm trying.

Steve can speak intelligently about every subject on earth. He loves learning, and it shows. He is in no way an intellectual snob; he just loves learning. That's infectious. We all should make it a point to love learning more. In the end, it makes our conversations grow deeper and broadens where God can use us.

My last bit of advice is to remember to stay encouraged. You matter in the kingdom of God. I said it before, and I'll say it again. Church work is not for the weak. It will test your resolve. All of us can have doubts about our direction. I know—I have had some long, sleepless nights. One that stands out in particular was in the earliest weeks of starting The Journey. It was very slow going, and I was getting frustrated with only seeing one or two visitors a week. One night, we got this e-mail. It was from a young lady who had attended our church only once, and we have not heard from her again. Let me share:

Good evening,

I had the pleasure of going to your church about a month ago for the first and only time. I came upon your church nothing short of a miracle from God. I was feeling very low one day, and while getting out of my car, I thought, I need a message from God to keep me going. When I went to my front porch, I found a flyer from your church. I immediately went to your website and began to cry. My prayer was answered. You see, I had just gotten married in February to my boyfriend of five years, and immediately after marriage, he started beating me. I didn't have any family in Colorado, and so I felt completely alone. I kept thinking that this was somehow my fault.

I summoned the courage to go to church that Sunday, and it was exactly what I needed. The sermon was clearly meant for me, from God. The pastor spoke of loneliness in our society. He spoke of the need for us all to reach out to others, and if we feel alone, to reach out to our family and community. I met the nicest person I have ever met that day. It was a young lady who sat with me the entire time. That sermon stayed with me the next week as my terrorizing experience continued.

Within a few days, I made the embarrassing call to my parents. I explained the situation and cried. They flew in that same day, moved me out and back home way up north. I want you to know that my wounds are healing, and I am okay now, and your church played a big role in that. You gave me the courage to reach out. I have found a great church here and am finding God in new ways. Although I will never be a member of your wonderful church, I want you all to know that you have forever changed my life in our one brief meeting. I just wanted you to know that. Thank you.

She went on to say a few more things that we will all forever treasure. That e-mail became a reminder that we are not the surgeons; we are the paramedics. Our job is to get people to God. We can help; God can heal. Remember that you are needed more than you know in your community. God called you. Believe it and walk accordingly.

Well, that's it, sports fans. I hope this helps and even starts some conversations. If you're ever in Colorado and want to visit, come on by. We'll even call Jim and see if he has some road kill left.

Rock on, my friends, and stay strong.

For More Books Coming Soon

by Michael Cheshire

visit

KnockOverA7Eleven.com

About the Author

Michael Cheshire is the senior pastor of The Journey Church in Conifer, Colorado. He is both a speaker and author. He lives in Colorado with his wife of seventeen years and their three wonderful children. To learn more about Michael or The Journey, visit them online at JourneyFoothills.com.

CPSIA information can be obtained at www.ICGtesting.com
Printed in the USA
BVOW021730200712

295804BV00001B/8/P

HOW TO KNOCK OVER A 7–ELEVEN AND OTHER MINISTRY TRAINING

by Michael Cheshire

Cheshire
Publishing

ISBN: 978-0-9853811-1-0
Printed in the United States of America

Cheshire Publishing 3/23/2012